PACE

a book ABOUT running

NOT running

AND taming my

INNER asshole

PACE

ANN MANDT HALL

Bulk purchase discounts, customized copies and signed copies are available by contacting the author through the website at www.ergorunning.com.

ISBN 978-0-9950905-3-8

For those on the run – may you enjoy the moment.

Much love and appreciation to my grandmother and mother.

Thank you for showing me what the courage to put yourself out there in the world looks like AND the incredible guidance on how to be a better red-head.

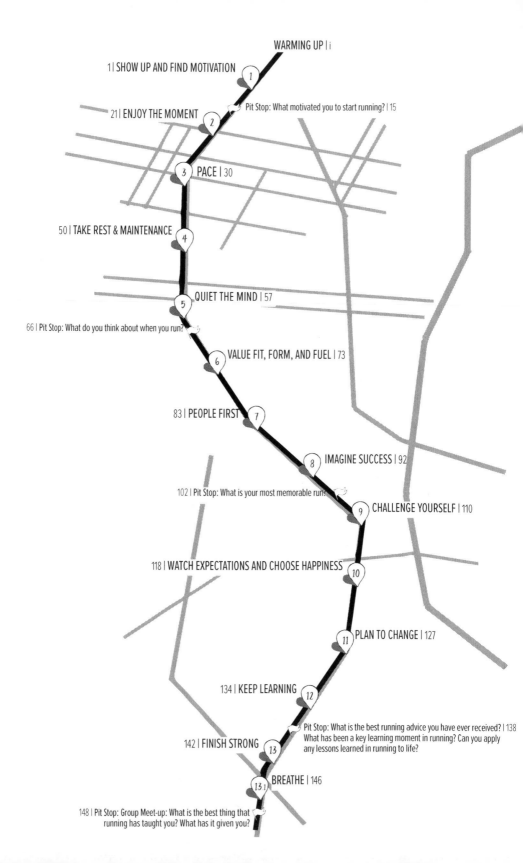

WARMING UP | i

1 | SHOW UP AND FIND MOTIVATION

Pit Stop: What motivated you to start running? | 15

21 | ENJOY THE MOMENT

PACE | 30

50 | TAKE REST & MAINTENANCE

QUIET THE MIND | 57

66 | Pit Stop: What do you think about when you run?

VALUE FIT, FORM, AND FUEL | 73

83 | PEOPLE FIRST

IMAGINE SUCCESS | 92

102 | Pit Stop: What is your most memorable run?

CHALLENGE YOURSELF | 110

118 | WATCH EXPECTATIONS AND CHOOSE HAPPINESS

PLAN TO CHANGE | 127

134 | KEEP LEARNING

Pit Stop: What is the best running advice you have ever received? | 138
What has been a key learning moment in running? Can you apply
any lessons learned in running to life?

142 | FINISH STRONG

BREATHE | 146

148 | Pit Stop: Group Meet-up: What is the best thing that
running has taught you? What has it given you?

CONTENTS

Warming UP

I'm 45 years old. At one point I thought I would never get to this age. I hoped I would, but I was scared that it just might not be in the cards for me. My late 20s and early 30s were spent sprinting through life at an unsustainable pace.

Tomorrow was always going to be the day I got my stuff together and would not worry so much or work so hard. Unfortunately, that day never happened until I was sitting inside a hospital emergency room watching people scurry around beside me. Minutes earlier, everyone had been so calm.

I asked the nurse closest to me, "Is everything okay?" She replied, "Your resting heart rate is in the 180s. We are scared that you are getting ready to go into cardiac arrest."

Well … that was surprising news! I won't go into the long story on how I got to that moment, but needless to say I didn't expect anything quite so serious. I asked the nurse, "What should my resting heart rate be?" The answer was around 60–70.

I'm not really sure how I remained calm at that moment because that is totally unlike me. Had I known that cardiac arrest meant my heart would stop, then I might have had a bigger reaction. Instead, I laid there a little lost in thought.

I wasn't worried about deadlines, a clean house, bills. I was worried about my kids. My daughter was only an infant. She wouldn't even get to know me. What about my son? He is on the autism spectrum and I am his biggest advocate. I come from a herd of people with anxiety disorder. I knew my parents and sisters would freak out when I told them about my heart.

That one moment of time brought a lot of clarity to me on how and why I should live. My heart didn't stop, and—thank goodness—within a couple of days they were able to get my heart into regular rhythm. The road to becoming stabilized was long, but I emerged determined to not sweat the small stuff. I used this event to set a new pace for myself in life.

This new path has not been easy for me, because life is life. I sit here today wrapped up like an Eskimo because my heater is not working. I'm on day four of waiting for the repairman. My dog has been driving me crazy because he is trying to "pass" half a pair of kid's underwear and a Barbie arm out his sphincter.

My sister called and said that she thought my mom's cat had been run over. She went to the road where she saw it, bagged it up, and took it to her house to bury. Turns out my mom was at home with both of her cats. This means my sweet sister has someone else's dead cat in her hand and now needs to try to find the real owner. Ah, life—expect the unexpected!

If you would have told me at age 35 that I would be writing a book on running in my 40s, I probably would have said, "Why running? Why not 'how to hug a shark' or 'how not to pee yourself skydiving'?" Any of these topics would have seemed similarly unlikely for me. Here I am though, 10 years later, filled to the brim with a love and passion for running—even though I spent most of my early years trying to avoid it.

When I think about life and running, I think about playing cards. I used to play Rummy with one of my friends. He always wanted to go out first. I would tease him, "You win the game by having the most points, not by laying your last card first!" Still, he always played with the same strategy, to quickly get rid of all high cards and go out. He rarely won. He was so stressed about being the one to go out first that I wondered if he even liked the game.

As silly as I used to find this, I came to see that I did the same while running. I would try to run a race as fast as I could without truly enjoying the experience. I eventually learned that I needed to redefine what winning a run would look like to me.

I also came to see that I did the same thing in life. Life is the greatest of endurance events. Getting to the finish line first is not how I want to end my game. How sad my grandmother would have been to know that I was sprinting through life, and at times not even enjoying it. With my heart, I came face to face with the finish line and this made me reassess everything important to me.

So here I publically admit, "Grandmother, you were right. This running journey has helped me remember all those lessons you tried to teach me, but I was too stubborn to really learn."

After my heart complications I told myself, "You know what? You need to rethink your racing strategy." Please note that this declaration didn't happen all at once, nor very gracefully. Picture me running with my shoes tied together carrying a piano, a horse, and a tire.

I finally figured out that I didn't have to carry such a weight, or try so hard. With time, I slowly put each item down and took the time to properly lace my shoes. Unburdening myself has been such an incredibly freeing feeling!

Some people have written about learning all they needed to know in kindergarten, or by watching Disney films. I learned, or maybe it is better to say I was reacquainted with, essential life lessons while running.

Trying to purposely slow down, take rest, and pace myself has been a challenge, especially when there are never enough hours in a day.

I admit that I am far from perfect in my journey for a more Zen life too. I continue to be a work in progress. Earlier today I was staring at the swear jar in my office. It's almost full. I probably should have been thinking something along the lines of remorse, but instead I was thinking of what kind of triathlon gear I might be able to buy with all the money that I have earned cursing. My morning and afternoon commutes alone have helped me fill half the jar. Thank goodness running now helps me cope with my everyday stress!

THIS BOOK IS MY PASSION

My family and friends are tired of me talking about running. For a long time I have tried to limit my conversations about running to those who I know run. I am sure my siblings would say—try harder, BUT... I can't seem to resist using running as an analogy to working.

Long before I began running, I was focused on the areas of pace, behavior change, fit, and fatigue in work environments via my career in corporate wellness and ergonomics. I feel that there is such a huge correlation between these areas and running. This is particularly true for the subject of PACE.

This book is a compilation of my thoughts and experiences gained while running. It includes a crossover between my work passion and my life passion, which when possible I enhance with research and the experiences of others.

I have taken all the lessons I have learned from other runners and myself and have applied it to my workplace. Most people understand why pace is important in a marathon, but ask them to pace themselves at work by taking small breaks and they aren't always so agreeable.

I also took all the research I had regarding pace and preventing fatigue in the workplace and applied it to running.

In a moment of clarity I realized that what I really needed to do was to apply key running wisdom to my type A personality life. Perhaps this is how I would get to the place I needed to be in order to attain my goal of better health.

I started by making a small list of things:

- Remind yourself to slow down; recovery is important to growth.
- Don't fight change, expect it.
- Focus on your race and not the race of others.
- Don't forget to enjoy the moment.

While running, I see people underestimate themselves and others all the time. How often does that happen in real life? What if changing your attitude and perspective in life could be as easy as it is in running?

As I made my list I also had thoughts about things like 'choose kindness' and 'put people first'. I made myself do a double take. Am I practicing these things in real life like I should? Am I practicing these things while running a race?

Perhaps I could not only improve my life by applying running principles. Perhaps I could improve my running by applying life principles.

I am constantly asking myself: WWIDR—*What would I do running?* or WWIDL—*What would I do living?* Each gives me a different perspective on the other, and allows me to adjust my actions accordingly.

 I BECAME A RUNNER IN MY LATE 30s

In the beginning of this project, I would tell people that I was writing book called, "How to run and not lose weight." I thought that I would get skinny running, but being that I am a woman now in my mid 40s and not so disciplined in my diet, that dream just never happened. Instead, running gave me a new way to look at life, and even to live life.

As much as I joke about this, I wouldn't change a thing. To be able to lace up a pair of shoes and leave my problems on the road has been life altering. I am not proclaiming I am now the Dali Lama of running. Quite the contrary, I am full to the brim with anxiety, and in terms of discipline—if you hold a donut in front of my face, watch your fingers!

My pendulum regularly swings from low confidence—"I probably can't finish a 5K"—to thinking I might be half ninja—"Hey, why don't we run up the stairs of the John Hancock Building before we have coffee and tour the city by bike."

The point is, I am not a super dedicated athlete, or Zen spirit, or even rational. I am an average person who dreamed of better health and to be skinny. My consolation prize was an amazing network of running friends and a clearer, stronger, and all around better mind.

I have been truly in awe of how much running parallels everyday life and what I've been able to take away from this super, sometimes awful, exercise.

I still joke about how horrible running is to do. I never ever thought that I could run. It still surprises the heck out of me that I can. The hurdle for most of us in running is our own mind.

When I talk with people and they tell me they can't run (physical ailments aside, of course), I often think of a Winnie the Pooh saying. Piglet asks Pooh, "What if a tree falls?" and Pooh replies, "What if doesn't?"

What if I can't run?
What if you can?

Some days I run 6 miles and other days I doubt my ability to even run one. No matter what, I know that even the best runners have difficult days. Every day I am competing with myself, and proving to myself, that I am tougher and more capable than I ever give myself credit of being.

When I struggle to run up a hill, I draw strength from the struggles I have overcome in my everyday life, like raising a child on the autism spectrum. The challenge of the hill soon looks small in comparison.

Every time I learned to push through those hard times while running, I became stronger and more confident. I can now draw on the experiences from past hard times to get myself through new hard times.

I have learned to adapt and appreciate the times when things are easier. When running up a long steep hill I always anticipate the relief and exhilaration I'll get from running down the hill. When that downhill finally arrives, I savor every moment before the next uphill.

Sometimes when I get anxious I close my eyes and imagine myself running downhill on the park trails. That feeling of being totally out of control, yet totally at peace, calms me. Somehow, I am willing myself to mentally get to a downhill in my life.

I continually draw strength in life from challenges I have endured in running. "Remember...when you wanted to stop and you didn't? When you didn't think you could, but you did?"

Mentally, I am now tougher and more resilient than I've been at any other point in my life. Running has helped this freckled-faced, red-headed, chubby girl with a birth mark on her face cope with anxiety disorder, stress, and poor self-image.

For so long I wouldn't even admit that I was a runner. Now, I don't even flinch when I mention I run to someone and they give me that great up and down eyeball glance. *I get it. I don't look like what you think a runner should look like, thanks!*

Somehow, not only do I like to run, I've now become dependent on it. I am the first to admit that I get grouchy if I don't get running time during the week!

I sort out my life's problems on the road. I clear my mind and find inspiration. It is where I challenge myself and gain confidence.

No other sport has ever given me so much mental space to fill. In the beginning that was the challenge:

- How do I occupy my mind on a one or two hour run?
- How do I quiet that negative inner voice that tells me that I can't do it?

During some of my first long runs, it felt like I was arguing with myself for darn near the whole race. The argument was always centered around whether I could or could not complete what I had committed myself to do. I was always grateful for the times I got distracted, and before I knew it another mile was gone.

Once I got more control over my attitude and head space, running eventually became therapeutic.

My family and co-workers would say I am an obnoxious runner. They are proud of me, but I don't miss the eye rolls when I proclaim I am going to go for a run, or when I show up to an early breakfast in full spandex.

On the obnoxious runner scale where ten is, "I have all the coolest gear, talk about running insanely, have zero visible body fat, act like running is always easy, post every run on social media and don't eat sugar" and one is "I do a 5K twice a year and carb load before and after"—I rate myself a five. *My siblings will disagree!*

I don't judge anyone else along this scale—I have occupied every spot on this scale at least once—with exception of having zero visible body fat. That would be great, but alas I continually choose my love for food over my desire for a better body.

As much as I love running now, I must confess one thing. When I think of running for the rest of my life I get completely overwhelmed.

Most times, I can only focus on the next 6 months to a year. For this reason, I always try to sign-up for races that are a couple of months out, as a security blanket to reassure myself that I won't fall-off.

I want to always run, but I still struggle with confidence at times. It is a lot of work and dedication to keep up running. I get scared I might stop, either by taking one or two weeks off and not picking it back up, or by injury.

There lies the core of my over-eagerness to always keep going. I'm scared to stop. It is not only the physical benefits I am fearful of losing. I don't want to give up my new perspectives and greater quality of life.

Luckily, my new perspective has led me to focus on choice. During those moments when I argue with myself, I always remind myself that happiness is just a choice ahead. I can change my situation or I can change my attitude.

When that fear of no longer running surfaces, I reassure myself with this mantra: "My life is better when I run, but if I can't run, I can bike. If I can't bike, then I can [insert activity here]". To be clear, I control my perspective and am willing to find the joy and life lessons in any activity.

WWGS: WHAT WOULD GRANDMA SAY?
Stop worrying about what you can't control and enjoy the moment.

MY STARTING LINE

I remember running super-fast three times as a child. Once, an adult yelled out "snake" at a camp fire. I sprinted away from the fire all the way home. Later, the adult commented, "I had no idea you could move that fast!"

Never doubt the ability of a child who fears everything. Still today, if something scary happens, people are going to look around and ask, "Where's Ann?" In the distance they will see my big bottom moving like it's on fire!

I have always made plans for worst-case scenarios—most of them have me high-tailing it out of there. So, basically, all the times I said I couldn't run (which were many), the truth is that I could. Deep down, when push came to shove, I knew I could muster up a quick sprint or long endurance run if I felt I was in danger.

What always held me back from running was that my mind was stubbornly locked in on this one thing—the internal voice that tells me that I am not a runner and I could never be one. I always defined a runner as someone who had this unique runner's DNA. From looking in the mirror, I clearly didn't have the right genetic code, so therefore I was not one of the chosen ones.

I never once considered that running was probably difficult to most everyone, in the beginning. That to become a runner, you need to work into it and train, verses this illusion that you just one day put on a pair of sneakers and run.

Honestly, starting like a normal person by entering a training program probably would have never worked for me, anyway. I don't like to be boxed in, confined by a rigid schedule. I feel suffocated when I can't "go where the wind takes me." I quickly become bored and direct my attention elsewhere.

Perhaps it's the internal struggle of the creative mind fighting against structure, which ironically is what my creative mind needs in order for it to be its most productive.

Anyway, I remember my grandmother once telling me that the master of all trades is the master of none. Her point was to always focus on one thing and do it well, and that is how you will advance.

The only problem is that her process sounded pretty boring to me, so my schedule typically consisted of a mix of this, a mix of that—yoga, swimming, running, biking, hiking, strength training classes, tennis, golf, zumba, and anything else that piqued my interest.

True to my grandmother's words, however, I have never been exceptional at any of these things, but I have liked doing them ... sometimes.

It has taken me a long time to become friends with running. Through the years, I've begrudgingly forced myself to run in an attempt to lose weight. If you would have ever caught me smiling, it was like they say about newborns—it was probably just gas!

Most of the times I did run, I would combine it with walking. Never had I started running outside and just continued until the end of the trail, not for any notable distance anyway. I didn't even consider this an option. I ran and walked. PERIOD. Running was horrible. I couldn't do it, I was 95% sure of that.

... until this one day when everything changed. The motivation to run found me when I wasn't even looking for it. I showed up and things fell into place.

After running a 5K without stopping, I was like a caterpillar emerging from a cocoon. I really surprised the hell out of myself!

My mind was so distracted that day that I forgot to think about how I couldn't run. A seemingly average sequence of events actually turned out to be the milestone that started me on my running journey.

No critter chasing me, I just decided to change direction by sticking with a friend when I thought they needed me.

Every year in Louisville, there is a race series called the Triple Crown, which consists of a 5K, 10K, and 10 miler. I signed up to do the series with the wellness group at work. Even though I didn't plan on entirely running each race, I couldn't resist jumping into the office banter regarding who was going to dominate the events. *Me!*

I had a solid plan:

1. Run like the beasts of hell were chasing me.
2. Stop and walk until I could breathe again and wasn't choking back vomit.
3. Repeat.

Mindset: These races would be epic, and I would probably win. *Well, at least the 5K. I am obviously built for speed!*

The morning of the 5K race I was looking super serious doing stretches and double knotting my shoes. My co-workers' time was spent mocking me.

About ten minutes before race start, I happened to run into my co-worker Denise—who was somewhat freaking out. All week on Facebook she had been posting that she was training to run her first race, and was nervous. She had planned to run with two of our friends, but she couldn't find them. She looked at me and said, "I didn't even bring headphones!"

In a one-minute time frame my brain did a quick assessment. The really insecure part of me didn't want the pressure to keep up with someone else. The inner asshole part of me wanted to get a good time and didn't want to slow down for someone else.

Usually I run-walk alone. Remember my epic plan?! The one where, when I won, all my co-workers who had been teasing me would be eating their own words and would be totally amazed by my stellar performance?

In the end, I knew I could never feel good about leaving a friend behind and that we should try to do the race together.

Typically, when a race started I would dart out like I was half Kenyan. I would quickly weave my way through the crowds like I was getting ready to set a world record. Within minutes, I would quickly fade AND then I would walk.

This race, Denise and I started the run at a much slower pace. People were flying by us, and this didn't seem to faze her. I definitely noticed, however, and felt the incessant urge to pick up the pace … but I had already committed myself to stick with Denise, no matter what.

What I also started to notice along the run was that, for once, running seemed fairly easy. When Denise got tired, we would slow down for a bit, but we always kept running.

Crossing that finish line was so exhilarating, and yet shocking at the same time. I actually RAN an entire race. *she jumps up and down* I'm not supposed to be able to do that!

I was so fixated on helping Denise that I never even thought about stopping myself. This was a first.

I look back at this moment as the "a-ha!" moment where I realized you don't sprint a 5K. Slowing down my pace to a speed where I was comfortable, and could get into a rhythm, made running enjoyable. I started to slowly learn that the key to running, for myself anyway, was to make it easy, then add speed.

Most importantly I realized that, maybe, I can run. Maybe I do have a tiny bit of runner's DNA in me somewhere, which helped me eek out that run. Surely, though, I couldn't sustain a run for longer distances—or maybe I could? My mindset was starting to shift.

By completing that 5K without walking, I gained a really tiny brick of confidence. Looking back, this one moment of time has served as a foundation point to help me in the ongoing battle with my negative mind.

Denise asked me to run the next race with her. I said yes, but 6 miles seemed like an impossible distance to sustain running. I really didn't think I could do it. I was nervous, but I thought, "Show up and see what happens." Worst-case scenario, I go back to my comfort zone of walking and running.

This race, Denise mentally carried me. We ran at a faster pace and Denise was running strong. I would describe my running style as frantic. I was running like we were lost in the desert, searching for water. When I wanted to stop, Denise would tell me, "Keep going."

I know I would have walked some if it wasn't for her encouragement. She helped me get through the mental points when my mind wanted to give up.

You should have seen us hugging and jumping up and down at the finish line. I mean this was "I won the lottery!" level of excitement. I remember looking over and seeing two of the younger guys from our work team looking at us like we were crazy. *Haven't you ever seen two middle-aged moms hugging and jumping over completing a race? Hahaha!*

We were just super proud of each other and ourselves. We stretched that mental rubber band, learning more about what we were actually capable of doing. It seemed impossible, but we did it!

How skewed it was of me before that first race, to think that I was doing something nice for Denise. The irony of the whole situation is that she did something even nicer for me. She taught me how important pace is, which led to me ultimately being able to do longer sustained runs.

At that point, that was the longest distance I had ever run at one time. In a mere six weeks, Denise and I went from running a 5K to a 10K to a half marathon. There was a 10 mile in that group of runs as well. I admit I walked a bit in that one. I ran too fast, too soon, and burned out. *It takes this old dog a bit to learn new lessons.*

I gained so many tiny bricks of confidence in my running ability during this time. I didn't believe I was actually a runner, but I was on my way. As I began to add other tiny bricks from running milestones, my confidence improved, and so did my mindset.

I never knew what was going to happen, and I wasn't sure if I was going to be able to do all the races. I just kept showing up—AND Denise kept showing up!

SHOW UP *and* *find* MOTIVATION

1

One book I read about writing said, "You want to be a writer? Start writing." The book suggested that in order to be a writer you should make a commitment to write 300 words every day, or at least for one hour. Even if you have nothing to say, show up and start writing about anything and everything.

The act of writing itself will make you a better writer and by showing up, something good will happen. When it comes time for editing, you might perhaps get rid of half of what you write, but then you are still left with the other half—AND you build confidence in your ability to write.

While writing this book, I can't tell you how challenging it has been to sit in front of an empty screen when I am just not feeling it, but I stayed true to the process half of the time. Half of the time I made progress.

Do you know how many times I thought, "*The hell with writing. I'm giving up on the book?*" Me neither, because I stopped counting at 1,000.

Do you know how many times I had a tough run and thought, "*The hell with running! I'm never doing this again?*"

The thing is, even when running gets tough, the more I show up, the better I get. Just like writing, progress is made through consistency and being present—AND I build confidence.

The pressure to perform a certain way on a run is sometimes almost too overwhelming for me. I have found that if I just concentrate on showing up, the rest will fall into place. I don't always have a great run, but I'm always glad I tried. The more time I spent running, the more comfortable and better I got at it.

After much reflection, mostly while running, I have decided that—for myself—showing up is the single most valuable thing I can do in running, and in life. Really, I consider showing up to be one of the most basic and fundamental running principles.

Showing up for runs is how you evolve and improve in running. It conditions you. It really is that simple, or is it?

There is a saying that, "Half the work is just showing up." JUST? Hahaha!

OMG! If you only knew how hard it has been for me to even get out of bed for some of these early morning runs. The bed is so comfy, but somehow I will myself to get up and get going, most of the time.

Wayne Gretzky said it pretty darn close to best when he said, "You miss 100% of the shots you don't take." This to me means that I have to keep putting myself out there, whether I am feeling the best or the worst about the day. Really, you never know how things will shake out. Some of my best performances have come as a surprise ... in less than ideal conditions.

Last year, I was chatting with another parent about school track participation awards. Our girls both received them and they were last in almost every race all season. We laughed, but then I got serious.

Their participation is a huge accomplishment! Imagine how hard it is to always show up to something when you continually struggle or finish in last place. It takes tenacity to hang in there and keep returning.

The girls laughed all season and had good attitudes, even as they were the last to cross the line. I am proud of them. I hope this experience leads to life lessons and growth. When you keep persevering, there is accomplishment in the end.

Not being the overall winner doesn't take away that accomplishment. Maybe this is a perspective thing. One of the beautiful things I have always loved about running is that I am always competing with myself—sometimes co-workers too—but mostly me. If I simply just keep showing up and putting forth the effort, I will evolve.

Pittsburgh Steelers' linebacker James Harrison made news when he made a public statement that he made his kids return all non-winning participation trophies. For a few weeks there were MANY debates where people argued that only the winners should receive awards.

I mean, I think we can all say that we know the difference in a 'we won the championship' award and a 'we showed up' award. These are two distinctly different awards that don't have to take away from each other.

I don't know if anyone truly appreciates a participation award like runners. Make the award shiny, make it fun, and runners will show up to your race!

These medals symbolize not only the hard work and dedication that we all put in to show up and endure, but also the sacrifices we make to train and prepare for the race. Everyone who crosses that finish line wins.

The more I talk to runners and hear their life stories, the more I am reminded that we often have no idea what others go through to simply show up and compete.

I have a running friend who was hit by a texting motorist while he was out doing a training run for the NYC marathon. Fast forward through five brain surgeries, dying three times, 1 month in a coma, losing a portion of his skull, and the months he spent in a wheelchair—now he can run again.

Can you imagine the joy and achievement he must have felt to do his first 5K after recovering from all of that? It must have been unbelievable!

More recently, he was in charge of a push-up challenge that I joined. Please tell me a good excuse that I could have given him as to why I couldn't complete the challenge. Too tired? My arms hurt? He literally came back from the dead and fought to run.

I often remind myself that running is a privilege that not everyone has in this life. I ordered a pair of running shoes online, and when I lifted the lid of the box these were the words written on the inside, "Get out and run while you still can."

Those words have mentally pushed me out of the door many times. *Why didn't I save that box lid?! It should be hanging on my wall!*

For me, showing up to run—or whatever—is important. I realize that more now than ever before. Showing up for running, others, work, and myself indicates that I am willing to put effort into these things, and that they matter to me.

Us runners—*see I am identifying as a runner*—sometimes put high expectations on our friends and family to be at our races. Some of these races are so special to us, we want to share the experience with the people we love.

I have seen so many conversations on running boards and in groups talking about the presence, or lack thereof, of our friends and families at events. I myself always had these fantasies of crossing the finishing line and looking over to see my family cheering for me.

It wasn't until I was 45 that I actually was able to experience that moment. I completed my first triathlon—1 mile swim, 25 mile bike, and 6 mile run. I will never forget pulling into the transition area on my bike and seeing my mom and 13 year old son standing there. I could not wipe the smile off my face. Someone even yelled out to me on the last mile of my run, "Nice smile!"

It was the first time they had ever shown up to one of my races. My son, being the ever stoic teenager, was totally unimpressed. I think I had been across the finish line for about 3 minutes before he asked when he could go home.

As we were walking to the donut area, I looked over at my son and said, "I can't believe I just did that. It was so hard!"... and then, waterworks. Watching me, he had a look on his face like, "Oh God! How do I make this stop?" He never again asked about when we could leave, and I think—but I am not completely sure—that I saw a little tear in his eyes. I absolutely cherish the medal I received on that day. I really do. I couldn't stop smiling, well, except when I was crying!

There have been so many races that I have seen loved ones cheer and greet runners as they cross that finish line. I have always found this to be very touching. I don't care if it is the first person or the last. That smile! That look of accomplishment! I love to people watch runners crossing the finish line and 'catch' some of that emotion—the laughs, tears, and unbelievable bear hugs!

As far as running goes, you just don't forget when people show up for you. Besides all the other emotions, there is a priceless look of complete surprise when a runner looks over and sees someone who they didn't expect, who has shown up for them.

My running friends have been some of the most supportive people in my running life, and also my personal life. Doing these things together, where we stretch our personal limits and break boundaries, has bonded us in a very personal way. Sometimes you need to lift someone up after a bad race, or sometimes you receive the most joyous hug in celebration of a well-run race.

My running friends have challenged me in ways that have led to me improving everything about my runs, because they knew I could do it, even when I didn't.

Just the fact that I know my core running friends will be at a practice run or race when they say they will be, keeps me constantly engaged and motivated. If I say I am going to meet you for a run, baring sickness and natural disasters, I will be there. How am I still running? My running friends won't let me quit. It's not even an option.

I bring this up because this is where running and life have merged together. This is where I have looked at my 'regular' friendships and wondered—am I showing up enough for people to things that really matter to them? Do they have things in their lives that mean as much to them as running means to me, and how can I show up to support them?

Certainly, showing up meant something to me far before I started running. I just didn't think about it much.

Many of us have at least one friend, sometimes a great friend, that has a show rate of less than 50%. You just come to expect that most of the time they are just not going to make it. You will get an excuse, or sometimes nothing at all, like the plans really never existed.

Those friends that do show up for life moments—whether in happiness, grief, or everyday normalcy—are extra special. We all have busy lives, so when they do make time for you it is certainly a bonus, even if all they send is a simple text.

There was a time in my late 20s when people showed up for me. Years later, I still have a deep appreciation for their effort and kindness.

I was getting married and at the same time my grandmother Digna was very ill.

I'll never forget when she was in the hospital and they put bootie socks on her. She asked the nurse, "Don't you have something with a little bit of a heel?" I had to find moments like this to laugh, because her illness weighed so heavily on my heart.

I actually moved the wedding to her town so that she could be there and be a part of the planning. I just couldn't envision my wedding without her, but unfortunately, she was too ill to make it.

After a long day of getting married, I took my first sip of champagne and exhaled. One minute later my dad told me that my grandmother had passed away that morning. She had held on with everything she had to be there for me for that day. I will never forget that moment at my wedding reception, so overjoyed and then completely gutted.

My Dad and my aunt lost their beloved mom only hours before my wedding and they still showed up for me. My Dad walked me down the aisle. He let me laugh and enjoy the moment, while he was completely broken inside. I went from the highest high of celebrating my wedding to the lowest low of finding out my grandmother was gone. My Dad celebrated with me at the wedding and then later consoled me when I learned about the death of my grandmother. I look back in awe at the strength he had to have had to do this, my aunt too.

People who had traveled in for the wedding, traveled back days later for her funeral. Outside the visitation room there was a line of people waiting to show their respects. I walked past the line talking to people, sharing hugs. I couldn't believe some of the people who showed up.

The lady who did my hair before the wedding was waiting in this long line to pay her respects to me. I had only met her twice. She said she read the obituary in the paper, and remembered how much I cared for my granny. I still tear up when I think about seeing her there.

Friends and family showed up for me during one of the best times of my life, and one of the worst—all in the same week. People I barely knew showed up for me. Their acts of kindness and support completely overwhelmed me, endearing them to me forever.

Putting this high value on showing up has been a blessing, and at the same time somewhat of a curse. It has led to me overcommitting and putting myself into complete exhaustion. It has also led to me not showing up, because I couldn't be everywhere at once.

This entire book is stitched with mentions of pace and expectations—mainly because this is one of my constant struggles. Running, however, has taught me to, "Watch your pace!" Does anyone else have to pace themselves at showing up for others?

This path of having too high expectations for being there for everyone has led me to not showing up for myself. There has to be a balance in there somewhere. You need to do things that ensure you care for yourself, while you are doing things for others.

Showing up for myself is probably the hardest thing I learned to do, especially as a parent. So much of my time has been spent focused on those around me that I have oftentimes neglected even my most basic needs.

I had to redefine what it means to me to show up, in order to alleviate internal pressures. Sometimes, for me, showing up is sending a text or a phone call. I now give what I can that is realistic. I still go the extra mile, but not every single time. It is not sustainable.

Honestly, this area of my life is such a work in progress. I get mad at myself all the time for not meeting my own 'too high' expectations. It is regularly one of the things I think about when I run.

A month ago I had one of the most important work meetings of my career. My work partner Hank had a death in his family and couldn't make the meeting. I received a phone call from him where he said, "I have watched you work and I have no doubt you will do a great job." This is showing up in my mind, not in the physical, but in the mental. He has been one of the most supportive and encouraging people I have ever had the pleasure to work with—and we live hours apart. *I need to be more like Hank, just don't tell him!*

Showing up to that meeting alone, or to a race for the first time, takes a willingness to put yourself out there in a very vulnerable way. I have found that the more comfortable I get with not caring if others see me fall, *or learn,* the easier it is to show up to other things that might be a little scary.

Just a couple of months ago I showed up to my first open water swim. On the inside, I had a giant scream face emoji. On the outside, I was the happy face emoji. It took everything I had in me not to ditch the wetsuit and take off running back to the car.

This is what I read on the internet, so it must be true—make the choice to put yourself out there and start showing up for any relationship or activity (work, running, writing a book), and you will improve that relationship or activity.

I recently watched a video on the internet about how showing up for your spouse, both mentally and physically, is the foundation of a marriage. I don't have a high success rate in this area (currently 0 for 2!) so I can't speak much about if this actually works.

I did used to get envious, however, when other people's spouses showed up. Every time that I got in from a long business trip, I would secretly hope that my husband would be waiting just past security. I also wished that when I crossed that finish line in an extra tough race he would be there. It never happened, but I guess I never vocalized how much that would have meant to me, either.

Showing up takes work, but this work is the start of all relationships. It shows a commitment to an activity or to a person. Most importantly, it means something to the people around you.

Now, if I mentioned how important it is to show up for work, you would probably say—"You think?!" Actually, I don't know what you would say, but that is what I would say.

I want to share one more story.

Someone in my immediate family (I can't name names in fear of retaliation, but it may be a sibling!) got fired from their first job in high school for not showing up to work on time. I can still remember how upset my grandmother was about this. She said, "I can never show my face at the Weiner Shack again."

The struggle many of us face is trying to find balance to do all the things, and to maintain motivation. I can't tell you how many nights after a long day of dealing with work and kids, I have flopped down on the couch and thought, "I don't have the energy to move from this spot." Some days I muster up the energy to power through, and other days … I just do what I can.

This chapter focuses on the two evil twins—showing up and finding motivation. They look so innocent together, but underneath they are as complex as macrobiotics.

Many of my non-running friends ask me, "Where do you find the motivation to do all that exercise, mostly running?"

My typical response is, "I have heart disease. I don't really consider that I have the option NOT to exercise regularly. Perhaps in a sick way, I am lucky to have this disease to push me on." I wish I didn't have it, but it changed my life for the better.

When your life depends on you exercising, you will be surprised what kind of time you can carve into your schedule. It is not that it is always easy though.

One of my favorite memes is a bear chasing a cyclist down a hill. The caption says: "Sometimes you find motivation, sometimes motivation finds you!"

The motivation to exercise will always be there for me because of my health. My motivation to run started with my friends. I would never have had the confidence and motivation to push through and run those races if it wasn't for Denise. She is someone who without question would show up and would also count on me to show up, too.

It was easier to push through the mental toughness of running when I was doing it with and for someone else, rather than myself. When Denise wasn't with me at a race, I would think about running for my grandmothers and my aunt who had all passed.

In the beginning, I was never truly alone because I was always mentally bringing someone else along. It took some time before I could just run a long race for myself.

During runs, I still focus on others every once in a while. If the race is meaningful—or extra tough—I dedicate each mile to someone special to me. It gives me motivation to endure in spades.

At the end of this year I ran the *Joggin' for Frogmen 5k* benefiting the Navy Seal Foundation, in honor of my favorite Navy pilot, my Dad. During the run, I was thinking of the strength and work ethic he instilled in me, in addition to how he has been such an example of how a man can be kind, loving, generous, and respectful to others.

I really can't believe that at age 45 I was able to break my own personal record for a 5K. Still goes to show that sometimes your best performance comes when you run with your heart.

This motivation has worked for me, but something entirely different may work for you. The thing I have found about the hunt for motivation, both in running and in life, is there is not often a singular solution for every person.

Be warned … I often get super nerdy and start talking about behavior change techniques with my industry friends. Basically, if you work in corporate wellness and ergonomics, you will be dealing with this topic a large percentage of the time.

We tend to have this conversation with ourselves: "They asked for help. I gave it to them. They didn't follow it. They have asked for help again."

"How do you help people help themselves?" That is the golden question we all want answered, so we don't spend our days hitting our heads against the wall. The truth is, so many of us struggle to find and maintain motivation—and the will to change.

Last week, I was talking to a young girl who was in all sorts of pain from working way too long on her computer. She was working full-time and going to college. Between the two, she logged over 11 hours per day on her computer. She was experiencing what she described as severe neck and back pain.

Each time I would offer a solution she would quickly offer me an excuse on why it could not be done. It was like a game of ping pong. I would hit a solution over to her, and she would

hit back an excuse. I would find another solution based on her excuse, and then she would serve another excuse back.
Finally, I just wanted to ask, "Do you want to be better?" The worst part was, I could totally identify with her. I have been her.

What works best is when a person decides THEY want to do it. I mean, when they feel the need to do something so great that they are able to weed through all the excuses and acknowledge that to accomplish their goal, they will have to make changes.

I usually ask people to write down what they want, why they want it, and how they plan on getting it.

Just the act of writing things down increases your commitment to the goal, and increases your overall chance of success by up to 42%.[1]

Now, if you are stubborn like me, you might just turn over that paper or misplace it sometimes, but still, you know it's there.

If you want a friend or family member to start running with you, nagging them is probably not going to work, at least not for the long run. Can I tell you how many times someone has lectured me on how I should be doing something? Lifting weights comes to mind. Organizing my house comes to mind. There are two choices—either argue with them or appease them and say okay. Neither is very motivating for me.

My neighbor is one of many who have been told by their doctors that he has high cholesterol and blood pressure. I can guess with much certainty that not all of these people went out and became runners the next day, like he did. Some may have had to have an actual heart attack to make any significant change to their lifestyle at all.

What I have found during my work is that no matter how good the intention is of the person or what their goal is, behavior change is not easy, not at all. Sometimes, we sabotage ourselves or make things much harder than they have to be.

The person most motivated in the beginning may have come out of the gate with too fast of a pace and unrealistic expectations.

When they did not succeed right away, they quickly lose their motivation to continue.

We often see this happen in running circles, too. People try to run too far and too fast their first time out. Many of us have been there.

In my work, there are three common types of people.

First, there are people who stick a toe in the water, seemingly to ease into a change. Next, there are those who jump right into the deep end of change, without even knowing how to swim. Lastly, there are those that refuse to even consider the possibility of getting wet. That last category is where we really need to WORK to earn our money!

These are extreme categories, so maybe you would classify yourself as being between two categories. I'm not.

I am the person who jumps right in, and then thinks, "What the hell have I done now?" I can honestly say that this has not always ended well for me. For instance, you may go to the salon to get a trim, and come home with a perm! For me, jumping right in takes a lot of the anxiety out of the experience. Sometimes, however, I need to pull back a little and pace myself into making a change.

Knowing yourself, and then coaching yourself based on how you react to change, helps. If you are hesitant to make a change, maybe you need to start more slowly and engage a friend that will have a positive influence. *Perhaps, they will talk you out of that perm!*

Self-control is thought to be something that is exhaustible, that we don't have an unlimited supply of. This makes it crucial to reward ourselves and go at a reasonable pace. Pace helps prevent burnout.

This is also why we encourage people in our programs to start small, so that they feel the results sooner and are subsequently more motivated to continue.

A good example for the need for pace is in marathon training. If you have never been a runner, it is probably a lofty goal to think you will run just over 26 miles. I am sure there are exceptions, but it is probably best to start with a 5K, and then train for sequentially longer distances. You get to achieve milestones along the way.

Now, you are probably thinking: *Wait! You just told us the story about how you ran a series of 5K, 10K, and 13.1 mile races within weeks, without much training!* Yes, but remember, that was me jumping right into a situation and then asking myself: *What the hell am I doing?*

Physically, it worked because I was in really good shape from interval training classes, which had built up my endurance. It also worked out because each of the smaller distance races served as a milestone. I felt so great after doing each, that it kept me motivated to reach the end of the series.

I am sure that if the 13.1 distance was our first race, the outcome would have been much different. Mentally, I needed the confidence boosts from the first races to help me believe that I could do it. I also needed the commitment and support of my friend along the way.

This has been a lot about running, but all of this can also be applied to life. That is the entire point of this book—flipping the switch between applying key running principles to life, and then applying key life principles to running.

I applied the way I started running towards the writing of this book. It was too overwhelming to think about writing an entire book, instead I just focused on small milestones, like writing one chapter at a time, sometimes even just writing a paragraph.

Along the way, when things became too overwhelming I reached out for a support system to get direction, affirmation, expertise, and accountability. I have found that, in many areas of my life, I need that encouragement and companionship while working to reach a challenging goal.

The bottom line on behavior change and motivation that I have found to be true is this: *We do what we want to do, and we make excuses for what we don't want to do.*

If there is something you want to do, make a plan. Write it down, put it where you will see it, and give yourself four weeks to accomplish it. If you start to struggle, ask for help, and draw upon your past successes to build confidence. Four weeks is a 'doable' length of time, and indeed has been proven to be a good length of time to reinforce behavior change.

Motivating ourselves is hard. It takes persistence. Approaching it with a "reasonable for you" strategy can make a big difference. Showing up is hard. It takes a willingness to invest in something and sometimes to be vulnerable.

Two of my all-time favorite quotes:

"When you're trying to motivate yourself, appreciate the fact that you're even thinking about making a change. And as you move forward, allow yourself to be good enough."
—Alice Domar

"I've always loved the idea of not being what people expect me to be." —Dita Von Tesse

PIT STOP

WHAT MOTIVATED YOU TO START RUNNING?

"You must be imaginative, strong-hearted. You must try things that may not work, and you must not let anyone define your limits because of where you come from. Your only limit is your soul. What I say is true—anyone can cook ... but only the fearless can be great." —Ratatouille

Aww … such profound wisdom from a movie about a cooking rat!

Every time parenting requires me to watch a children's movie, I am not too enthusiastic. I even somewhat dread it. I don't know why though, because ninety percent of the time the movie is good and I walk away inspired by the message.

I loved the message in Ratatouille: *"Not everyone can become a great artist; but a great artist *can* come from *anywhere*."*

Running transcends economic factors, age, and race. When I walk into a running store and the elite runner asks if I need the shoes for running, I confidently reply, "Yes." If the rat from Ratatouille can cook, then I can run. It may not look like their run, comparatively. It may be slow. It may not even be that far. But I can run.

I came to think, if I can endure parenting, death, etc. … then I can run around the block. It took me awhile to get to that mindset. I never thought I could, and then I did. I have talked to many other runners who have felt the same way—and then they did!

Not every running story is made up of the things people dream about, like the epic run of *Forest Gump*. He was sitting on his front porch and then he took off running. "I just felt like running that day for no particular reason." He went to the end of the road, end of town, end of the county, end of the state—he ran to the ocean and then to the other ocean. For no particular reason, he ran for 3 years, 2 months, 14 days, and 16 hours.

He said his mama told him, "You have to put the past behind you before you can move on." He thought maybe that was what his run was all about, and then he was done. That was the end of his running. He fit a lifetime of running into that period.

Many of us everyday people don't have such a dramatic story. We decide we are going to force ourselves off the couch to run, maybe to lose weight or to try to get into a better state of health. Some of us just know it's time for something to change. Running is a chance to take control of our lives. Some of us don't choose running, it chooses us.

Take Jack Taunton for example. His dream was to be a professional football player. When the realization came that his dream would not happen, he turned to running. With that one decision, a life-long passion and commitment bloomed into something super special. In fact, Jack has a story that many of us amateur runners would dream to have—one of training and mixing with world-class athletes, one of BEING a world-class athlete. The man has finished 63 marathons, half of which were under 2:30!

You know my story. I am an average runner at best, but I would like to think that I have heart that exceeds my ability. I just had to find it.

The following is a collection of stories and comments from runners who I have met along my journey in running. These people continue to inspire me every day.

Thomas, 48; Lexington, KY

I was athletic in high school. After that, however, the only thing I curled were 12 ounces. I had gotten up to around 250 pounds.

I wanted to lose weight and I was dating someone. I joined a gym and started using the elliptical. My girlfriend said that if I really wanted to start losing weight, I should run on the treadmill. She was living in California and I was living in DC Metro. We would line up 5Ks to run when we would meet each other. Of course I wanted to build off that, so I did some 10Ks, half marathons, and eventually some full marathons.

Half marathons were my favorite because the training wasn't as intense as for marathons, and the recovery time was much shorter. I could rest a bit after one and still be good for the rest of the day. In 2015, I set a goal for 15 half marathons, so I ended up racing or maintenance running most of the year. Now, I do a lot of triathlons.

I have stuck with running because of the people I meet. I

have met so many people, and there all these groups on Facebook dedicated to running and triathlons. That is the exciting part— the social perks of running! I enjoy running groups where you meet to run 3 or 5 miles, and then hang out and socialize over a drink afterwards.

I had gotten to the point in life where all I was really doing was working. I wasn't really doing anything, nothing exciting anyway. I am a balance type of person now. I want to make sure that I have something else, outside of work, so when I have a bad day, I have something to look forward to doing. That is why the running groups or races coming up mean something to me. They give me balance. That is what makes me happy.

Jaclyn, 35; Salem, MA

I was going through a rough time in life. My parents' marriage wasn't doing well, my roommate at the time had moved out and we no longer were speaking, and my current boyfriend had broken up with me. I figured I would try doing something that would be more painful than dealing with my personal problems, so I started running. I joined my local *Team In Training*, started training for a half marathon, and I haven't stopped running since.

Lucy, 54; Louisville, KY

I was new at Eastern High School as a sophomore, and I found a deep pull in my heart to run. I discovered that when I ran then, and still now, that my mind, body, and soul were in alignment.

Sarah, 45; Portland, OR

My Dad has been running as long as I can remember. I ran cross country for one season when I was in 4th grade, but I didn't really enjoy it, and my Dad never pushed me to do it.

Fast forward to when I was 38. I had been doing a little bit of running, nay sprinting, with my dog Lucy to help her burn energy, but I really had no desire to run any distance. One summer, I went on vacation to the beach. I love walking on the beach, but I decided to do some interval running/farklets on the beach as well. A couple days later I was swimming laps in the hotel pool and a complete stranger asked me if I was a triathlete. I laughed and said, "No, I really only like to swim. I hate to sweat." That short conversation, however, started me thinking about it.

I was already swimming and running. I knew that a gym at home was doing an indoor triathlon, which was a really awesome way to get started. I still wasn't sold on running, but I signed up for that race one month later. Three weeks after that, on Christmas day, I broke my hip. That began my real motivation to run, but not having done the triathlon before that happened, I didn't think I would have ever found my path to becoming a runner. The desire to run was my motivation to heal as quickly as I could. I ran my first race seven months after I broke my hip, and it wasn't pretty. I was beat by a race walker and several kids. However, I was very happy to be back out there running. Nine months after I broke my hip, I completed my first triathlon.

Mike, 36; Dayton, OH
In my late 20s I got to a point in life where I questioned if I wanted to keep living. I was depressed and had started to seclude myself from others. I was the heaviest I had been, weighing 350 pounds. One day while I was on duty as a policeman, I was called to a house to talk to a family regarding a theft from their vehicle. I got so winded walking up just two steps. The look the family gave me upon seeing this left me with the feeling of worthlessness. It felt like they were thinking—*How is this guy going to help us?*

Around this same time, a family friend who had battled cancer for many years was diagnosed with cancer again. I visited her in the hospital and admired how she could have such a positive outlook and attitude in life, even though she was battling something with no cure. I had a problem I could fix and decided based on these two events to make changes in my life.

I made a total change to my diet, and started doing cardio at a gym where one of my friends was a trainer. I lost 100 pounds in 5 months. After I had lost the first 80 pounds, I joined my aunt for a 5K in Cincinnati. I was still heavy, but I was able to run. I loved the positive atmosphere of the race, and decided to keep running. I ran a 10K later that year, and eventually started training with friends for a marathon. Since that time, I have done many races including several half and full IronMan events. I absolutely love the atmosphere in the multisport community, everyone has a story! You open up to people on the marathon course when you talk to them. And it's pretty amazing and often brings a tear to my eye to hear other people's story. It's still fun to see myself progressing and my times improving.

ENJOY
the MOMENT

Before my running journey actually started, when I was walking and running races, people would remark, "Oh, you did the race. Did you run the whole thing?" I always felt a weird mix of emotions after one of these encounters.

It seemed like a simple good-natured question by most, but the question itself felt stitched with judgement by others. I felt like they thought that by walking a part of the race I had done less than everyone else.

At the time, I never dwelled on this too long because, after all, running wasn't my 'thing'. I exercised when I had time. The bulk of my activity was done inside a gym and at interval training classes.

During those first sets of races with Denise, she talked me into running a half marathon. Her goal was to run the entire race, so I sort of made this my goal too. I say 'sort of' because I wasn't sure I could actually run such a long distance. I told myself, "Either way, I would be good." Really though, deep down inside I wanted to be able to run the whole thing—more than I probably even realized then. I just lacked so much confidence in myself to commit to the goal.

Right before the race I became nervous and insecure. I quickly came up with a new plan, to start switching between walking and running at mile 4.

I can still see Denise staring at me blankly as I quickly recited the new plan. Her face sarcastically said, "Yeah, sure you're going to do that." Minutes later, we started to run.

After what seemed like a very unreasonable amount of time, I finally turned to Denise and said "I can't believe we haven't reached mile 4 yet." A guy running beside us started laughing. He pointed to his watch and said, "We are at the 6.5 mile point."

How the hell did I miss those giant mile markers?! While I was reflecting on how I had gotten to that very point, I just kept running in cadence with Denise.

We got separated in the tunnels leading into Churchill Downs, which was just about mile 8. It was quite chaotic and when we emerged into the infield, I realized I would probably not find her.

The infield was congested with people. So many runners had slowed their pace to run through the historic race track. Many stopped to take a picture, using the iconic double steeples as a backdrop. People were laughing and hugging their friends as they took group selfies.

I didn't dare stop, not even at the water stops. I wanted to make sure I could say I ran the entire race. I tried to take a selfie while still running. You can imagine how that turned out—part of one arm, part of my face, and quite blurred!

A little later, a text came through on my phone. I couldn't resist the temptation of looking at it. I glanced down and saw a note from my sister Alice, "I am so proud of you." I was just closing in on the 10 mile marker. I was completely overwhelmed. At that very point, I knew I was going to do it. I teared up.

I ran the entire race. I remember laying in the grass after the race wondering how we just ran so far, and how we would possibly make it back to the car. My feet hurt so bad. I was so happy though … now when people asked me if I ran the whole race, I could say yes.

Little did I know there was a second question to follow once you answered yes to running the whole race, *"What was your time?"*

Great! Not only do I have to run the whole race, now I have to achieve a good running time. What is a good running time anyway?!

After that race, I ran several races using my continued stubbornness to commit to never stopping, no matter what. This also began my unhealthy fixation on my race time.

As I became a much more experienced runner, I slowly started to unravel a realization. My time doesn't matter. It's okay to stop and take a water break, use the restroom, or take a picture. Doing these things does not make you less of a runner, or negate all your efforts to run a good race. A good race is determined by your own standards, not what others think.

It took me a long while to get to this point. One of my running friends said they had been talking to a very seasoned runner. This runner had given her some key points of advice. One of which was, "Always take a water break on long races."

In fact, he said, "Stop, drink the water, and then continue." This was a huge contrast compared to how I had been living! I wasn't taking stops. And if I did, I tried to drink water from a tiny cup while running. *I am going to make a video series showing all the people trying to run and drink from a cup one day.* I typically wore more water than I drank!

Now, a seasoned runner had given me permission to stop and have a drink of water. It must be okay.

At the same time, research I had been exposed to at work supported this runner's statement. Those who take small 'pit stops' are often the best performers, not the worst.

Keeping your body properly hydrated is key to having a comfortable race. I had been taking this run thing a little too literally. Just because you stopped to drink a glass of water, doesn't mean you did not run the whole race.

Around this same time, my friend Todd volunteered me at the last minute to take another friend's race bib for a trail half marathon. I had just ran a half marathon the weekend before, so I was less than eager to enter this race. I said no, but three days later I was standing among 100 runners in the wet grass waiting to run up and down the hill trails of Seneca and Cherokee Park.

I stuck with my friend Krishna the entire race. He was in his late twenties at the time, and like many people in their late twenties, he drank too much and slept too little the night before a race.

We started running at a very leisurely pace, and based on how we were feeling neither one of us ever stepped up the pace. At one low point, we were running up a very steep hill and someone passed us speed walking. That was a nice laugh. We paused at every water and food station for a leisurely stop.

Krishna: "Look at all this food!"

Ann: "I haven't had peanut M&Ms in years!" as I casually stood there eating them and scanning the table for other treats.

People working the station were looking at us with eyes that said, "Shouldn't you guys be running?"

Out of the 100 runners, we were among the last five to finish. Krishna hung beside or behind me the entire race, except for the last 500 yards, when out of nowhere he darted ahead. *Congratulations Krishna, you finished number 96 instead of 97!*

It sat in my mind for a long time that this was the best race I had ever done. My music playlist had malfunctioned, and somehow it ended up playing easy going music. The scenery was beautiful. The run was challenging, but we went at a comfortable pace. I was with my friend. We laughed, and I dare say we had fun!

All the other runs with better times were good, but not like this.

Months later, my childhood friend Sarah posted an account of one of her races on the Oregon Coast. After I finished the story, I read the first comment on her post. It gave me pause to reflect.

I reread the story looking for the paragraph referenced in the comment: "As I was running my heart out, I watched other racers heading toward the water. I realized they were taking their time and collecting sand dollars. Who has time for that when you are running a race? There's no time to waste! Keep your mind on finishing this leg!"

I read the post comment again: "I enjoyed reading about your race Sarah. Good for you and your team. Sounds like a beautiful area, and maybe next time you'll stop and gather those sand dollars."

That one comment hit home for me. In racing and in life, maybe I was too focused on goals and not enjoying the journey itself.

We all want to beat our own best times, but it is equally as important to enjoy the overall experience. The people who stop to take a picture or collect a sand dollar are living in the moment and enjoying the race on their own terms.

I want to be like that, but it doesn't come natural for me. My attitude usually is tinged with, *"What else could I be getting done right now."* I actually have to work at NOT working. I have to assign a greater value on those moments—the ones where you step away from intensely focusing on a goal, to pause and reflect.

I have to re-program myself from that German work ethic that has been ingrained in what I do. I need to see those times as a gift and not as a moment of laziness.

How often do I just step back and appreciate the beauty of normal everyday life? Metaphorically, I need to dip my toes in the water more often, capture the moments, and savor the downhills of everyday life.

Ironically, for half my life, a Ziggy corkboard on my wall has said in large-print letters, "Stop and smell the flowers." Why did this message not resonate with me until now?

My grandmother, who was a lover of sunsets, always said, "Never miss a sunset." It was one of her greatest pleasures. I loved that idea, but never took it to heart. I wish she was still alive so I could tell her, "I get it now." It was never so much about the sunset, but rather the need to pause, reflect, and enjoy life. To appreciate the spectacular things around us every day. That, and a sunset really is amazing!

Thus came my new LIFE and RUNNING motto: When someone asks you if you enjoyed the race, plan on answering 'yes'.

I still have those races where I try to challenge myself and improve my race time, but I also have new methods for approaching longer races.

No matter how fast paced my song race list is, I will make sure the song *"Solsbury Hill"* by Peter Gabriel plays. This song is my reflection song, and one that reminds me to enjoy the moment. I tune out the minute it comes on, and start taking in my surroundings. I think of one memorable/enjoyable takeaway from the race.

Here is the best surprise, I have clocked some of my fastest miles while listening to that song. In that moment of reflection, I relax. I stop making things so hard on myself and I get lost in the moment. I have more comfortable runs, and better control of my pace.

That song once came on when I was running through the roads of Keeneland. Horses were running in the rolling fields beside us. The sky was beautiful. I was thinking about how in love I am with my home state of Kentucky. I can only say it was a majestic moment. Several people had moved over to the fence to take pictures of the horses. I wasn't exactly in the mind place of being able to come to a full stop during the race yet, but I really slowed down to take a picture. *It counts!*

I replayed that moment several times as a fantastic moment, and you know what? After the race when I looked at that picture I realized I had been running up a giant hill. I didn't even remember the hill. How did I not remember running up that huge hill? It seems like a hill I might complain about at the end of the race, but I didn't even recall it as part of that moment!

If I can block out that hill and feel like I am flying, then I have transcended.

This planned time of reflection and enjoyment has helped me so much. I now practice this on regular run days at home, in order to reflect on the day or week.

Sometimes, special moments appear on their own, and other times I am forced to see through rain and high winds to create a positive takeaway.

I figure this is about as close to meditation as I am going to get. This is different than thinking out problems. This is focusing on the positive and the beauty around me. It helps to lift my spirit from whatever is going wrong in life, and focus on what is right.

Now, the more difficult thing for me is practicing this in my daily life. My daughter's freckles, wiggly tooth, and giggles are things I experience every day. I need to remember to stop and mentally record these moments.

> *"Enjoy the little things in life, for one day you will look back and realize they were the big things."* —Robert Brault

Whenever I read this quote I think of stringing beans with my grandmother on her porch. Such a simple mundane task, but if I could go back in time, this is where I would go. It wasn't always a perfect time, or at the time it didn't seem perfect.

My grandmother would send me down to the garden with a giant bucket to pick beans. I would complain about this child cruelty and how they would all be sorry if I was eaten by a chicken snake.

I would stand at the edge of the giant garden while my grandmother would scream from way up at the top of the hills/

porch, "Just go get the beans Ann Wilson. Nothing is going to get you." I would dart in and out of that garden like I was running for my life. I could hear my grandmother laughing all the way from the porch as she watched me.

After I had picked the beans, my grandmother and I would clean them and string them on the porch. We talked about everything and nothing.

Strangely enough, I feel really at peace when I string beans now. I look forward to it every summer. It is probably the one dish I make for my family that I put so much love and heart into cooking. When my kids won't eat them, I can hear my grandmother laughing on how they are stubborn just like me.

Once, I forced my son to try a green bean and he projectile vomited on me. I still have a feeling my grandmother had something to do with this. I did things like that all the time while I was under her watch. I still won't try okra because it looks ugly, and if she was alive today she would probably still be mad about that.

This ritual has had so much meaning to me. I strung beans with her so many times. Even as a young adult I would run from the garden screaming while my grandmother watched from the porch laughing. I can 100% say that I would endure the creepy, snaky garden with the horrible little straw scarecrow a thousand times, if I could only be back at this same place with my grandmother.

My grandmother really perfected enjoying the moment. She worked so hard, but she always had time to sit on her porch and just 'be'. She coveted her sunsets, her jug of water sitting in the sun steeping with the tea bags and sprigs of fresh mint, her feet propped up on the lounge chair, and the surprise visit from a friend just to chat.

Taking time to relax, reflect, and appreciate is so important. I really wished I had learned earlier to do this more. Not just for my own quality of life, but also for my kids. I need to teach them to pump the brakes in life, and simply appreciate the moment. Everyday life has meaning.

> *"Be happy for this moment. This moment is your life."*
> —Omar Khayyam

PACE

3

If you run, then you know how important pace is in order to achieve a comfortable and sustained run.

We have all seen runners sprinting at the start of the race, only to pass by them later as they are barely able to keep running, watching them walking or heaving at the side of the road. You know I have more than my fair share of these stories! These runners get caught in the moment and start too fast, then quickly burn out.

In the beginning of my journey, when I thought it was too difficult to run an entire race, it really added up to be a pacing issue. I was running faster than I could sustain for the entire distance. This made the experience of running a struggle and overall unpleasant. My only solace in running at that time was the thought that maybe I would lose a pound.

It takes experience to achieve that perfect pace—the pace where you run at optimal efficiency and speed, and can still finish strong. It also takes planning to look at what is coming and adjust your speed accordingly so that you have energy reserves when you need them. Sounds pretty easy and straightforward … nope! Even the best runners still have their moments. *Or so I hear!*

I helped to coach a *Girls on the Run (GOTR)* team in Louisville, KY that had a mix of third, fourth, and fifth grade girls. My guess is that most of the girls in our group joined for the social part, and just tolerated the running. I say this because I heard at least a couple exclaim, "I don't like running!" And due to the fact that they nicknamed me, the coach who ran with them, 'the witch'. They said it was because my laugh sounds like a cackle, but I'm just going to go ahead and say it was the running—*for my own self-esteem!*

Each week, we trained for a 5K that would take place at the close of the season. On the day of the race each girl was required to have an adult running buddy. A casual adult runner probably thought, "I can do a 5K run, no problem!" What they probably didn't expect is that when you run with this group of girls, you are introduced to an intense pace of interval runs.

These girls take off at a high speed sprint, racing each other. They then stop and walk fast for a few seconds as they stare each other down, before taking back off again. Play this on repeat. There was soon a field of battered adult running buddies heaving and struggling to keep up.

There is nothing like extreme examples to provide opportunities to hold a mirror up to ourselves and evaluate how we live. That run was ridiculously funny and I had to admit to myself—I have run that way before as an adult. Not as extreme, and I most certainly didn't add a cartwheel, but I have done my fair share of the chaotic sprint and walk. By the end of one of those runs, my legs feel like they are on auto-pilot and I can barely move!

Now, I know some people love this method of interval running, *I still do it once in a while for a high calorie burn workout*, but I was solely doing that because I couldn't sustain a run.

When my daughter Charley Ann first started running cross country in Kindergarten, she was barely hanging in the races. It was not rare for her to finish last or second to last. Besides being easily distracted, she too would gas out early and then barely be running at the finish.

As she progressed on the team, all of this improved. By her second year she was in the middle of the pack. I think part of it was conditioning, and the other part was the experience she gained on the runs. She knew what to expect, and her body unconsciously adapted. Keep showing up and your body will eventually evolve, right?

I didn't push her, but I could see her pushing herself. Not to win mind you, just to be able to run with a friend.

I was so proud when I saw her run the first meet at the start of her third year. She had now transitioned into a longer distance run, which would be a mile. It was hot and humid, Kentucky style. The girls took off for the starting line before I could even think to tell her to take it slow.

I anxiously waited to see how she was hanging in there at the .25 mile point. She seemed to be running slow and steady, with one of her best friends.

It took a while for them to get to the .75 mile point, but here the two came, still striding along together. They looked relaxed, like they could be having a conversation while running. This was in contrast to some of the other girls who were holding sides and crying. *We have all been there!!!*

In conditions most adults would not want to run in, they held their own and ran a comfortable race. They finished in the back of the pack, but as her grandfather would say, "It was perfect in every way!"

I watched with pride in how she evolved. Sure, she ran slower than many of the other girls, but I was not watching her struggle anymore. I wanted to yell out, "That's right little ones, make running easy and comfortable for yourselves and the speed will come with time and experience!"

Chris, the coach who trains the cross country group, always says, "Make your last half of the race your fastest time." I needed to hear that as much as the kids.

Watching both of these groups shed light on my own issues with pace. I began to dig around a little on the Internet. I read an article from a master long distance runner who gave his best advice on having a successful run. It was simply this: "When you want to take off—hold back." He repeated this statement three times, to represent the first three quarters of a race. In the last quarter, he said, "When you want to take off—go!"

It was at this time when running a race began to drastically change for me. I had evolved in my running to take water breaks when needed, and to start out at a comfortable pace so I that could gradually speed up and finish strong. Essentially, save the sprint for the finish.

At the same time I was going through this evolution in my running, I was heavily involved with the subject of rest breaks and fatigue prevention in the workplace.

Ironically, the way to prevent fatigue at work is to establish a good pace and to take breaks when needed. It was the exact same thing I was focused on in running.

This realization has given me a lot of pause to reflect. In running, people take pace serious, not so much at work. People shrug it off as if breaks are totally unnecessary, as if they have no control, even though most do in some way.

My passion over the last 18 years has revolved around getting people to physically move more throughout the day at work. Scientifically speaking, I have focused on static muscle fatigue caused by sitting or standing too long without a posture change. When I hear employees say they are hesitant to get a glass of water or take a bathroom break in fear they will look like slackers, my heart cries a little.

In the last three years, I have expanded my work to spotlight other types of fatigue, especially mental fatigue. I realized very quickly that getting people to see the value of mental breaks would be a much tougher uphill battle, than the comparatively simple task of making people take physical breaks. It made the second task look like a fast flat course!

As I researched the subject, wrote articles, and spoke at events about the value of taking breaks and avoiding the onset of fatigue, I couldn't resist bringing running into the conversations. In my perspective, it was a perfect analogy.

Most people, runners or not, totally get how important pace is if they wish to achieve the best outcome in a run. Not one person has ever argued that point with me. I am waiting with great anticipation for that day. Closing arguments have been prepared by the person who learns everything, including the value of pace, the hard way.

Anyway, the more I learned about fatigue and breaks, the more I started to apply all my findings to my own life, including running, work, and general everyday living.

I took everything I had learned about mastering pace in running and applied it to my work. I then took what I knew about mastering pace at work and applied it to running. Finally, I took all this information and applied it to life in general.

Please don't let me over simplify this in what I am about to tell you. This 'ish' is hard. Sometimes, I hit a stride with managing pace in all areas of my life and it feels like magic, and other times, like mixing writing a book in with a full-time career, I go off-course. When I say off-course, I mean—standing in a field in the middle of nowhere screaming hello, wondering where the hell everyone else is.

Look, many of us have work days where we are working intensely at our computers, not taking breaks, and are under a great deal of stress. It really can't be avoided all of the time.

At the end of a day like that, we are exhausted. We didn't do any heavy physical activity, rather we worked too hard, for too long without breaks. For many of us, this means that when we get home, we crash.

If this happens every once in a while, that is one thing, but if we repeat this pattern every day it takes a toll on our health and our quality of life.

In my late twenties, this is how I lived—most the time. Long intense days at work without breaks. I sat at a computer for hours, with very little movement. I had a long commute, in lots of traffic. I rarely had the energy to do anything else on weekdays, especially exercise. I came home like a zombie.

Fatigue decreases our ability to respond to situations and zaps our energy. It is the enemy to our productivity. Yet, many of us are programmed to go, go, go. We see this as being super-productive and ignore what it does to our body.

The effects of fatigue on the human body can manifest in the form of tiredness, headaches, body aches, and irritability. It is often the combination of multiple types of fatigue (mental, eye, static muscle, and muscle over-use) that can lead to complete exhaustion.

A good coach manages fatigue in order to enable their athletes to achieve peak performance. They strategically plan workouts, which incorporate days for the body to recover. They also tend to the mind by talking with their athletes about topics such as accountability, encouragement, and support.

Can we apply those principles to life? Should we?

Science has shown that one hour of running each day is not enough to undo all the damage we do to ourselves by sitting most of the day, every day, and by putting ourselves through continued days of high stress with no breaks.

To disrupt this ongoing cycle, we must coach ourselves to manage fatigue by balancing activities and pacing ourselves throughout the day. It's that simple, but not simple at all.

This very day, one hour before a big meeting, all three of my dogs, *they have now been renamed the fur assholes*, came dashing into my house covered with shit from head to toe. Head-to-toe, people! I didn't plan on interval sprinting around my house and giving impromptu dog baths in the middle of my work day.

The skill of pace is not one that comes easy. Pacing yourself in running is one thing, and surprises will happen there, too—stomach cramps and shoe problems, to name a few. Pacing yourself in life is an entirely different animal—there's traffic, sick kids, tree limbs down, and any number of other 'surprises'.

We can't entirely control the day, only how we react to it. When I am working to pace myself, putting in the effort at least, I remind myself to slow down and take small breaks along the way. I now put more value on downtime.

That busy day where you have zero time for breaks is probably when you can benefit from them the most. You will be more focused and have more energy in the long run.

Let's think of running. How do we pace ourselves? The answer varies depending on distance, course difficulty, environmental factors, and personal health. Many factors need to be considered in order to find the best pace for a good, safe, comfortable run; rather than a run where you end up puking a mile from the finish. *I'm still waiting on pictures to surface!*

If we continually sprint through days at work without breaks, our endurance is bound to suffer. The top runners are not necessarily the most aerobically conditioned, but rather the ones who have mastered pace. They run at top efficiency, which is distinctly different than top speed.

Please allow me to put on my nerd hat for a second, and really delve into the subject of pace.

A study of elite performers ranging from chess players to athletes concluded that more rest can maximize achievement.[2] This goes against what many of us practice. We arrive at work, focus on the task at hand, and go as hard as we can without break until we become really fatigued.

Sadly, some estimates show as many as two-thirds of office workers eat lunch at their desk.[2] Employers tend to see these people as the hardest workers, but what they are doing has been shown to be counterproductive. Going without breaks exhausts us, and the result can be an increasing lack of focus and reduced quality of work.

Top performers, by contrast, tend to practice in focused sessions lasting no more than 90 minutes. They work in bursts, taking frequent breaks to ensure recovery and avoid exhaustion.[2] This structure supports studies that conclude that performance deteriorates during long periods of continuous work, but can be reversed by taking rest breaks.

Another study looked at race car drivers, again a place where pace is important. Surprisingly, the most successful drivers had more pit stops, not less. These pit stops were not attributed to the need to service the car, but rather to provide a mental break for the driver. This study highlighted the importance of taking small micro-breaks from intense mental focus, in order to improve your mental focus over the long run.

Each and every day our bodies give us signs that we are becoming fatigued. Once we become aware of these signs, we can then respond in a way that helps us avoid fatigue and better pace ourselves.

Here's an example that I use at work: You know that antsy feeling you get when you have been sitting too long? That's one sign that you are experiencing fatigue.

You can fidget and shift around in your seat, but the only thing that truly alleviates this discomfort is the muscle movement you get from standing up and moving around. Movement increases blood flow to fatigued muscles, and re-energizes them.

Let's say you repress this desire for movement, and let the static muscle fatigue continue to intensify throughout the day. What does this do to your body?

Imagine yourself driving on a 9 hour road trip. How do you feel when you get to your destination?

There is no tremendous physical activity, but the majority of people will be extremely tired due to fatigue.

You experience static muscle fatigue from holding the same sitting posture for so long, with only small opportunities for movement. To add to this, you most likely have mental fatigue from the monotony of the drive and the need for extended focus. If you are in heavy traffic, or have crying children—dramatically increase the mental load. Your arms and hands are also likely tired from gripping the steering wheel.

This is what makes me sad, some people's work environments closely resemble a long road trip—sitting for hours without movement in a closed space, intense focus, and repetitive arm work. Replace the traffic and crying kids with work stress, deadlines, customers, and co-workers.

There is good news: if you can show up for yourself to try to manage fatigue, even just half the time, you will begin to optimize your performance. This in turn will give you more energy and comfort, for running, work, and life!

At the end of this chapter I have included some tips for preventing fatigue. I mostly use these in my work environment, but they can also be applied to life and running.

The way we 'live' at work has a huge impact on our home life and running life. If you can control physical and mental fatigue at work, you will most definitely see the benefits in other aspects of your life.

I have talked to people who have increased their energy levels and decreased their discomfort. As an added bonus, some have reported more patience at the end of the day. This is not a promise, just a report!

If it sounds like I am selling something, I am not. I'm sharing what I have felt, seen, experienced, and learned. And as usual … some of it has been the hard the way. I was going 100 mph—in a 25 mph zone—in life, fueled by a type A personality and anxiety disorder.

My mentors have asked me, "What is the one thing you want readers to take away from this book?" Hands down, it has to be putting a value and respect on pace in your life. If one person could avoid the long list of problems and struggles I have been through, then I've been successful.

Here is how I now TRY to manage my life.

Every week, I look at what is coming up. Sometimes, I have to adjust the scheduling to even things out a bit. I look for opportunities to get in a run or yoga or something that will help me sustain a hectic pace, by giving me a refresh.

I work to have more realistic expectations about what can really be accomplished in a set amount of time. If I always compromise my mental health and well-being as a trade-off to completing an over-filled schedule, then I need to reassess.

There are times when I know that I have over-committed, so I adjust the intensity of the things I do. I make a compromise with myself. I can still do these things, but maybe I shorten the duration, or re-evaluate how I do them.

Here is a really small and simple example.

I love the *Run the Bluegrass* race in Lexington and look forward to it every year. When I finally went online to register last year, I realized that the race was on my daughter Charley's birthday. I thought about canceling, but I felt guilty because I had put together a team and recruited others to join us, including my sister Alice.

Lexington is half way to my parent's houses so I decided to combine the race with a family birthday celebration. While I was doing the race, my daughter went to her grandmother's for a special birthday sleepover.

To pace myself for the entire day I decided I would really take it easy on the run. This was to be a leisure run so that I would have plenty of energy left to celebrate with my daughter. I had to quiet that inner competitive drive, and summon all the strength of my inner turtle.

I gave myself time to recoup after the race, but skipped the usual brunch with friends to meet up with my daughter.

This change might seem really simple, but in the past I would have gone hard on the race, then quickly jumped into the car for the hour car ride to get to my daughter as soon as possible. I would have filled the day with as much 'fun' as possible, to over-compensate for the fact that I missed some of the day. At the end of the day, I would crash.

I have evolved now to look beyond the pace of the moment, to look into what pace I need to sustain to be successful for a full day or week. Not only am I less stressed and happier, the people around me are, too!

Adjusting for the day/week is easier than adjusting for life. Sometimes we get caught in this cycle of work, and if you are a parent, possibly lots of kid activities. Before you know it, years have raced by and we are going at full sprint through life.

I recently read an article about an attorney who went a year and only took one day off. I thought, "This is insane!" but then I realized that my first salary job didn't 'award' vacation until you had been with the company a full year. They also required salaried employees to work a half a day every Saturday. For one year in my late twenties, I worked a 6.5 day work week with no vacation and only the very basic holidays.

I was in terrible shape that year. I gained about 25 pounds and accomplished very little in my personal life. I had headaches that were so severe that I was sure I had developed migraines. All my family lived out of town, so I didn't get to see them often. I was depressed. When I got a chance to escape from that job, I did.

There have been multiple surveys and studies that look at Americans and their lack of commitment to vacations. One study reported that 54% of Americans left vacation days unused.[4] On average, that amounts to three to seven days per year, left unused.

Can I have everyone's vacation days that aren't using them? Please! Actually, I have cashed out on vacation days too, where you can take the extra money instead of the time. Guilty! It seems almost funny now, but it is not.

Check this out: "Women who don't take regular vacations are anywhere from two to eight times more likely to suffer from de-pression, and have a 50% higher chance of heart disease. For men, the risk of death from a heart attack goes up a third."[5]

When employees are questioned about why they don't use all the vacation, some cite money, others cite fear.

According to the study: "66% of employees feel that their company culture is ambivalent, discouraging, or sends mixed messages about time off."[4]

Some people say they have so much work that it isn't even worth taking vacation because so much more will be waiting for them when they come back.

I completely understand each one of these reasons. At times, I have dealt with them all.

I got caught in this lifestyle of being fearful of what managers or other co-workers would think of my performance if I took too many breaks during the day, or time off when I needed it.

If I could go back in time I would tell my then self to stop stressing and be confident in your work. Just like running, you can't always strive to live up to too high expectations just to avoid judgment. Just because others set unhealthy standards for themselves, doesn't mean you have to adopt them, too.

I was talking with my friend Chris about this over a post-run tea. We both agreed that oftentimes management acts as a pacesetter for those around them.

Chris works in operations for a large retailer. At one location, he had a boss who never took lunches or breaks away from his desk unless it was for a 'quick smoke'. In return, this is what Chris and the rest of the team did as well, minus the smoking. It was their everyday work life for years.

Less than a year ago Chris transferred to another location and his new manager was quite the opposite. The whole team went off-site for a full hour break. At first, Chris wondered if this was wasted time, but he noticed he had more patience in the afternoon and that the employees got along better. It was a much happier work environment, and the performance of the department was comparable to the other store.

He took the time to have some mental down time from the stress of retail. He took time to be social and engage with other employees about things that had nothing to do with work. This time had a positive effect on his general well-being, as well as on his relationships at work.

Another friend of mine works a joint job. Basically, he and another co-worker do the exact same job parallel to each other, thus they can be compared to each other on an apple-to-apple basis in terms of performance.

The other person arrives to work early (5 am-ish) and stays late. They even come in on their off-day to be seen and get some things done. If you watched Seinfeld, this is akin to the George Costanza model of working. Get there before the boss and leave after the boss.

At first, my friend let his co-worker set the bar (pace) at which the job should be done, but then he said enough is enough.

It is hard to reign back that inner competitiveness and drive. He had to ask himself, "What am I gaining from this behavior?" It was like chasing someone on a hamster wheel. If you ask yourself, "Why am I doing this?" and the answer is, "Because the person in front of me is doing it!" you may find some clarity.

His quality of life and happiness were deteriorating, and he wasn't getting anywhere.

After 'jumping off the hamster wheel' he became happy being at work again. His performance measurables on a normal schedule were the same as for his counterpart. He also started to notice how disgruntled his co-worker was at maintaining the pace she set for herself.

Bottom line that both he and I learned from this conversation—be careful when you choose a pacesetter!

Working longer does not make you more productive, and it does not make you better at your job. Just like running as far as you possibly can each time you run, doesn't make you a better runner. Overworking, just like over-training without recovery, is shown to have negative effects on both health and performance.

As I progressed at work, I finally started to change a couple of 'pace' things. I went against the norm of my co-workers and decided I would no longer be taking red-eye flights. One of my male counterparts dubbed me the office 'diva'. Still, I stuck to the plan. I agreed to travel, but I was no longer willing to push myself to extremes.

Imagine this lifestyle. You work all day, then head to the airport. You fly through the night and get home early in the morning. You go home, shower, and then head back to the office. How productive do you think I was after that? Have you seen the studies that compare one night of sleep deprivation to excessive alcohol consumption? I maybe got two hours of interrupted sleep, especially since there is rarely a direct flight home for me.

I have kids. I can't crash when I get home after work. The effects of missing a whole night of sleep and going so hard stuck with me for several days AND I knew I was less productive in all areas of my life when I did. I now refuse to put myself through that anymore, at least regularly. Every once in a while, I make an exception when it is crucial for meeting a specific deadline.

I can usually take an early morning flight and have a rested mind, enabling me to work as I travel. I tend to be much more focused and productive than when taking a red-eye flight.

I never consider out of the office time wasted, at least not any more. Some of my best ideas have come to me when I was away from the monotony of my desk. This includes time on long flights, car drives, walks, and runs.

Several years ago, I took a few days out of the office to go to a festival of random speakers here in Louisville, named the *IdeaFestival*. This was long before I was thinking about pace, but a tiny seed was planted that maybe I should be taking my vacation as a method of developing personal growth and recovery. It made me take a very significant pause to evaluate how I live.

Stefan Sagmeister, a well-known artist in New York, fully

convinced this Kentucky girl that taking long breaks from work are essential to stimulating creativity and re-igniting our passions.

He talked about looking at the way a typical person lived life. Chunks of time in the beginning set aside for school. A large chunk of time in the middle of life for work, and then a small chunk of time (let's say 8 years) at the end of life for retirement. His thought was, "What if instead of following this typical schedule of life, you could take the 8 years of retirement time at the end of life, and mix it into the middle of life?"

He tested his thought by going on a year-long sabbatical. He was so enthusiastic about the results. He claimed to return to work so re-charged and creative. The inspiration and ideas that he got during his time off is what he credits for making him even more successful than before.

He now takes a year off every seven years. During this time, he does not take work from clients.

This man, who seemingly is very different than me, inspired me. I knew it was far out for me to take a year off, seeing as I have young kids, but at least I could start by taking vacations.

In reflection, I had done a poor job of utilizing my vacation. Some years I took all of my vacation days but I used them on sick child days, sick days—*of course I caught it too*—snow days, or getting things done at home. Sounds like some real inspirational time, right?

In addition to my paid vacation time, we had the option to take an additional week off of work unpaid. That next year, I took all my vacation time, PLUS I took an extra week of unpaid time at Christmas. I worried I couldn't afford it, but everything was okay. It was totally worth it!

This was me just sticking a toe in the water, testing time off. Testing a reduction in money.

I knew I needed to make bigger changes. My son was in the middle of being diagnosed with dyslexia, this was in addition to a lot of other struggles such as anxiety disorder and sensory issues. His self-esteem was starting to suffer. We were forced to remove him from the school he loved and place him in a special needs school. A heart breaking moment was when he told me he was stupid and that he didn't like himself. He needed me.

Lots of work, lots of travel—including overseas travel—and lots of family stress. I had to say STOP! I was sprinting through every day in what felt like horrible conditions. It was not sustainable.

I have a heart problem and a child who needs me. I knew I needed to make some drastic changes. I needed to work less, travel less, and be there for my family.

I asked my company to go to a four day work week. The company reluctantly said okay, but that I would lose the majority of my benefits and my job as the manager of the department. I think at the time, the decision was hard, but I deemed it important for my family and I.

The company allowed me to carve out my own job, so I was able to focus more on workplace ergonomics and wellness, which is what I love. After I made that change, I never looked back. It was the right thing to do.

I used my one day a week as my sabbatical day. Sure I cleaned house and did mom things, but I also did things for myself. I took an art class. I started to get myself back.

I found a couple of companies that I could do freelance marketing projects for when they needed them. I started to actually make more money than I did before, and under better conditions.

Fast forward a year or two, and I said goodbye for good to that original job. I took a leap of faith and began to work part-time for a Dutch company. I still had my freelance clients. I knew I might make less money, but to live life on my own terms for a couple of years would be totally worth it.

This was as close to a sabbatical as I was going to get. I got to work at home, setting my own hours. I had an opportunity during non-peak work times to devote to my own projects, like this book. The uncertainty of everything made me anxious, but I could always remind myself there would be a cubicle waiting for me somewhere if things didn't work out.

I made a list of all the projects I really wanted to do 'someday', and then told myself that 'now' is the time. Pick one project and go.

For two years, I tasted freedom. I also developed a deep respect for my Dutch co-workers and their attitude on work and the value they put on breaks.

They never asked me to sacrifice my personal health to save money. They also respected my time as my own. I would tell co-workers before I went on vacation, "You can call me. I can still handle that." They would reply "Ann! You are going on vacation. Don't do any work."

This was a totally new concept for me. I have worked for European companies for the past 17 years. All our European counterparts took a summer holiday and a long Christmas holiday. They also had extended time off in addition to this time. Most took 6–8 weeks off, plus holidays, every year. On the American side, we rarely followed suit.

Three years ago was the first time since college that I decided to take a long summer holiday. I took two weeks off in a row during year one, and three weeks the next year. Most of my friends would comment, "It must be nice." Okay, it IS nice, but it didn't come without sacrifice. It was unpaid both times. I just made it work. This year, I didn't take any vacation during the summer. It just didn't work out—so I know I can't have this ALL the time, but some of the time is still nice.

Other times in my life, it would have been difficult to take that time off, but I think I could have still made it work. I could have just tightened the wallet a bit for a couple of months. Just a week off in my own home then would have been fantastic.

I am training myself to respect my time more. If I don't do this, I can't expect others to do it.

Similarly, pacing myself running is not easy, but it becomes trivial when I think about the journey I have been on in order to find a comfortable pace in life.

When I have trouble breathing and get uncomfortable in running, I slow down. When I have the same occurrences in life, I used to keep going. Now, I do my best to slow down and pause.

I have made running harder than it needed to be. I have also made life harder than it needed to be.

I want to scream at my former self, "Stop hitting yourself! My God! You are trying to sprint a marathon wearing a 50 pound vest!"

"Slow down, simplify, unburden yourself. Have less and do more. Take vacations and don't stress about it. Go out with your friends." This is what is I've found to be important.

"In the end, it's not the years in your life that count, it's the life in your years."—Abraham Lincoln

I could find a hundred quotes to hang on my wall like that. They are great, but like my Ziggy poster, in time they may just fade into the background.

So I made my own. To me, from me; to remind myself why I must pace myself through life. It's my motivation.

In my bedroom on a picture of my kids, the words I live by: "They need you to be your best." - Ann

If I ever waiver, these words are what brings me back to reality and reminds me to pace myself. I love to work hard, but I can do that smarter and more efficiently when I realistically pace myself. This helps to ensure I am a better me.

RESOURCE: SIX TIPS TO HELP YOU AVOID FATIGUE AND PACE YOURSELF FOR IMPROVED HEALTH AND WELL-BEING

1. Move more: Try to not sit or stand for too long. The rule of thumb is that you should have some movement every hour. This doesn't necessarily mean moving away. If you are at your desk you could simply stand to take a phone call. Ideally, focus on creating opportunities for movement throughout the day.

2. Take a screen break: I am staring at my computer for hours. I am taking a break from the computer to stare at my phone. Tonight I will rest by staring at the TV. See where I am going here?

Staring for long periods at digital devices is a cause of eye fatigue. WebMD estimates that this affects about 50%-90% of computer workers and is responsible for up to 10 million primary care eye examinations each year.

Some simple things to help prevent eye fatigue—take breaks from screen time, even if it is just looking 20 feet ahead for 20 seconds, and blink more often.

3. Schedule micro-breaks: Water cooler small talk is grossly under-rated. It gives you a chance to have a mental break, stretch your legs and have some social interaction.

Don't worry if you think you can't take a break. Breaks from sustained activity as short as one minute have been shown effective in restoring performance while at the computer.

Studies have shown that scheduled breaks were generally more effective than leaving people to take breaks at their own discretion.

4. Pace your day: That week where you just don't have time to exercise or take a break is probably the time where you need it the most. Schedule downtime to lessen stress and reboot. Consider both personal and business activities as you pace yourself for the day/week.

5. Watch your posture: Your posture and body mechanics while at the computer have a huge impact on your comfort and fatigue levels. It is really important that all your equipment are positioned in such a way so that your body is in a neutral posture. This will put less strain on the body. Even in the ideal posture, your body needs time to rest and recover.

6. Avoid muscle over-use: Muscle strain can cause a lot of discomfort and lead to a more serious injury. If you use one muscle group repetitively look for ways to take small breaks to allow recovery.

take REST & MAINTENANCE

4

I guess these races wouldn't be any fun if we all ran at the same pace. We have to go at the pace that works best for us. My pace is not the Olympic men's marathon pace of around a 5-minute mile. I would be very lucky to clock a 10-minute mile pace for that distance. A lofty goal for some, is mock turtle pace for others.

Last year my trail running buddy Kevin was badgering me about going slower. He said my spirit animal was a turtle. He sped off before I could remind him that the lifespan of a rabbit is maximum 12 years, compared to 80 years for a gorgeous turtle. Now who is winning?

It is hard not to push ourselves to the limits sometimes. Who doesn't love a good challenge? Don't think I haven't dreamed of beating Kevin in a race. It is easy to get goal-driven when running. Many of us grew up with coaches yelling at us to push ourselves harder. "Pain is weakness leaving the body!"

Turns out pain is really our body saying slow down, I need recovery, or worse—I am hurt. Telling yourself that your body isn't ready yet or needs to sit this one out is frustrating. Out of everything we do as runners, or non-runners, we must respect this vessel we have been gifted to travel through life in. It is our body. Not that I have always done this—I have not!

I have already shared with you that I pushed myself too hard at times. I have struggled with running pace, work pace, and life pace. I have also had to work at pacing my body.

Some of my friends struggle to find a day or two in the week to exercise. I struggle to find a day to rest. I don't like having a rest day. Resting is boring.

I want to run when the weather is perfect. I want to go to spin class if my friends are going. I love to run or bike or interval train or yoga or ...

My whole life of over-committing and over doing it boils down to one thing: I don't like missing anything.

I reluctantly settle on at least one rest day per week. I guess I am addicted to exercise, in some way. This is me loosely admitting it. I am dependent on it for stress relief. I just feel so much better when I exercise AND I can eat more. That is a big part of it, too.

My body reminds me to slow down through aches and pains. If I am too sore, I know I need to ease off and focus on recovery. I don't always want to, but I think of the old adage for those who don't take the rest they need:

"You can't pour from an empty cup!"

This is in line with, "You will be the fittest person on the side-lines come race day."

Rest and recovery fit together like this super tricky illusion puzzle. You think when you aren't doing things that you aren't progressing. This is the great illusion, because if you actually did do things you would be hindering your progression. Not doing things during periods of rest and recovery, propels us forward. It is just so hard to believe at times.

I so wish our bodies had a maintenance light, much like our cars. It could show warning lights about inflammation after a race, indicating muscles that need to be rested. This would be very clear and straightforward and take all the ambiguity out of the situation of when to rest and when to go. There would also be no guilt. Someone would ask, "Can you run today?" "Nope, resting light came on. Legs need a recovery day." Who could argue with that? *Someone on social media, guaranteed!*

As I have met runners and cyclists on my journey, I have observed a couple of things. The more advanced and skilled athletes will taper their training before a race. This doesn't mean total rest, this means slowing your regiment down and having some days of just really easy movement.

When you are in training mode, it is very difficult to take a rest day. It's almost like your body adapts to depend on this output of energy. One of my dear running friends was telling me that her withdrawals from running are really intense. She will see others running when she can't, and she gets legitimately angry at them. They get to run and she doesn't.

I am always a little scared that I will risk losing my hard-earned fitness. The truth in science, however, disputes my mind and tells me that giving my body a break actually gives me the best possible chance for success.

Recovery or tapering gives bodies a break from normal training volumes to let the muscles heal. It also allows your glycogen stores to increase by as much as 15%. Glycogen and fat are two primary fuel sources. When you allow time to rest and recover before a race you will, in theory, arrive at the start line feeling as fresh as possible.

Many of the articles I have read on rest days pertain to weight lifting and how taking a day from working a muscle group is really important, not just for the muscles to recover, but to grow.

I always run stronger when I take a day or two off before a race. Taking a couple of days off is, however, no comparison to taking weeks or months off. When I have an injury I am like a kid on a road trip—Are we there yet? Can I run yet? How much longer? How much longer now?

One of the fastest and most consistent runners I knew can now no longer run. After a surgery and time to heal, he was forced to switch his routine to biking or swimming. This change has been devastating to him. I mean this guy ran every day, EVERY DAMN DAY! He concedes, "I overdid it. I wish I would have cross-trained. I wish I would have run on grass more."

It's easy to beat ourselves up after the fact. Let's face it, he is one of many who has done the same thing. I don't know any runner that hasn't pushed themselves too hard a time or two, *or a thousand*. It is hard to distinguish the difference between what is pushing us to be stronger and improve, verses what is pushing us towards injury.

I have taken his experience as a reminder to myself to ease up when I know I need recovery. Of course, rest for me sometimes means that I reluctantly switch from running to yoga for a while. The good news is that I am as flexible as a hippo, which means I can always use work in that area! At least I feel like I am still moving forward.

Non-runners will look at a runner who is limping around proclaiming they are getting ready to go on a run like, "Buddy, wake up! You need to rest. You are setting yourself back."

Ironically, the same person judging the runner could be the person who shows up to work with a high temperature and body aches knowing they are coming down with a cold. This almost always turns out to be counterproductive because it typically elongates the recovery time and exposes others in the company to the illness.

Doctors see a lot of worsening symptoms because people will not take the time they need to stop and recover, just like sports injuries.

One doctor commented "what they don't understand is that they're actually a lot sicker at the end of two to four days than they would have been if they had just taken that first day off and let their body fight the infection."

Ideally we could all take the time we need to recuperate during an injury or cold, but sometimes this just isn't possible. It is at these times we must really use our pacing strategies to slow things down and get as much rest as possible.

WWGS: WHAT WOULD GRANDMA SAY?

Grandma would definitely say, "It's time to rest." She probably wouldn't even let me watch TV, so that I might actually sleep. She would make sure that I was hydrated and had proper nutrition. To have either of my grandmothers around to take care of me for just one day sounds like heaven. You can't replace a bowl of soup made with love.

Alas, at some point, we have to learn to take care of ourselves. What if we treated ourselves like we would our children or how our parents, better yet grandparents, would treat us?

What would I do if my child had a 101 degree fever? A twisted ankle? I certainly wouldn't be pushing them too hard.

Do I care for myself less than I care for them? Pretty much. I need to show them how to respect themselves, and this is done through actions, not words. As I stated before, they need me at my best. If that is my goal, then I have to use restraint and put energy into recovery when I need it. I'm not saying I always do this, I am saying I am a work in progress.

During the writing of this book, I developed plantar fasciitis and sciatica. I was forced to take a couple of months off from running. This time can only be described as '#@$!'

It was so frustrating not being able to run. After a week of repeated RICE (rest, ice, compression, elevation), I hobbled in to a sports doctor. He gave me the standard anti-inflammatory pills. When I didn't progress, I did physical therapy, acupuncture, massage, and visited the chiropractor. When I told the chiropractor what I was doing, he jokingly replied, "You are not a professional athlete, Ann!"

I know this, but it is hard for me to sit around. I am a very active person aside from running, and I was in pain. The physical therapy and stretching routine really helped, as did the other things, especially acupuncture. I did eventually have to taper my treatment routine because of cost and time. Sigh!

I learned a lot though during my short period with the physical therapist. If my symptoms start to appear—even a little—I immediately go to a more advanced stretching program, and also rest from training on hills and speed.

Of course, there are runner's groups for lots of support and laughs. If you have been through injury as a runner, you will totally get this conversation. It pretty much sums it all up.

Running Friend 1: *My doctor said, "You can start walking, slowly, and on flat surfaces. We'll get you started on a course of physical therapy." I replied: "So my 10K trail race next weekend ... can I still run?" The doctor stood there with a look that said, "Really?!"*
Running Friend 2: *Sounds like the talk I had with my doctor when I found out I had pneumonia, just days before my last marathon ...*
Running Friend 3: *And this is exactly why I don't go to the doctor!*

I thought about getting a tattoo that says, "Let yourself rest." That, however, seems a little over dramatic for the situation. Do I really need a tattoo to encourage me to rest when I need it?!

I know WWGS. She was a lady of leisure. She would say, "Books by the fireplace; tea watching the sunset; naps in hammocks on a breezy day; watching waves come forward and recede with toes in the sand." My aunt, another lady of leisure, would add, "Coffee and crossword puzzles on the back porch by the garden; feet propped up, good conversation and a glass of wine at the end of the day."

Now what would my Dad say about this? He would say, "Do you really have so few problems that you are upset because you get the luxury of having a rest day?"

This from a man who finally has chosen to PARTIALLY retire at the age of 84. He played on a basketball team until age 70, AND still he is better at resting and recovery than I have ever been.

I can take a picture of his body print that is embedded in a giant leather chair in front of a television in his bedroom to prove it. He raised three talkative daughters, so he has spent a great deal of time recovering, *seeking shelter/hiding*, in the solitude of his room.

Rest and recovery is the maintenance our body NEEDS in order to recover. Again—it is okay if you rest, even for an extended time.

Please do not feel guilty or lazy or like you won't be able to start again. You CAN start again and you WILL start again AND you will be stronger for it. YOU know what your body needs, allow yourself that chance to take it.

"Take care of your body. It's the only place you have to live in."
—Jim Rohn

5
QUIET *the* MIND

Forty-nine times out of fifty I can talk about my kids and be completely fine. There is that one time, however, when I start talking about my kids and I simply tear up. Out of nowhere, I get caught by emotion as if I suddenly just realize how much they mean to me, or how proud I am to be their parent.

I do this with running too. I'm always gabbing away about running, and then out of nowhere it hits me. I tear up with that sudden acknowledgement that running is a beacon of light for me as I navigate through the darkness of life.

Running is my companion. We have our good and bad times for sure, but these events only help to strengthen our bond. Really, I guess it's silly to think of running as a person, after all, I know it's an activity. There is a closeness there, however, that you get from hitting the open road and really getting to know yourself. Turning everything else off and working through problems and challenges, and basically just talking to yourself.

I bring myself down. I lift myself up. Sometimes, I think of nothing more than what is right in front of me, other times I reflect on life. All this happens to the cadence of my two feet.

Running has been the catalyst for me to turn off the world for a moment. Somehow, over time, I had forgotten what it was like to just 'be', in silence.

There are so many distractions in regular life. I have often avoided what I needed to deal with in my personal life. I achieved this by packing my schedule so full that I didn't have a chance to think, or even breathe. Any time not spent engaging with others or at work, was filled with noise from either TV or radio.

When I first started running I would crank up the loudest, fastest, and angriest music—this was all to drown my personal thoughts and reflections. I didn't want to deal with the mental part of running. I didn't want to hear my own voice or think about things that had upset me.

It's hard to run away from yourself, though. Sooner or later, the silence comes and we find ourselves staring alone at our inner selves.

> *It doesn't interest me what you do for a living, I want to know what you ache for. It doesn't interest me how old you are, I want to know if you are willing to risk looking like a fool for love, for your dreams, for the adventure of being alive. I want to know if you can live with failure, yours and mine. It doesn't interest me where you live or how rich you are, I want to know if you can get up after a night of grief and despair, weary and bruised to the bone, and be sweet to the ones you love. I want to know if you can be alone with yourself and truly like the company you keep in the empty moments of your life.* —Jon Blais, IRONMAN

I love it all, but that last line is everything. Getting to that place where I can be alone and be okay. That is the gift that I have given myself through running.

Over time, something beautiful happened on my running journey. Running became natural. I don't have to think about it. I show up and just go. The world turns off, and my mind turns on. My favorite is to run a course that I run often, like the scenic loop at Cherokee Park. I instinctively know every curve, incline, and decline of that path. My body goes onto auto-pilot.

I have often said that the park is my church. I find peace on even the most aggressive runs, especially running through nature on the trails.

The road is not only a place for my mind to rest, but also provides me with a time to clear my head. There are times I think through things that are lingering in my mind, and allow me to come to a place of resolve. If it can't be resolved on the road, I can make a plan to resolve it in life—and soon. Carrying extra mental baggage weighs me down.

I can't even remember how many times I have said that I love running a course with hills. These hills have become one of my great metaphors for life, and give me so much to think about. Dig deep and take on the challenge of the hill/mountain, and then enjoy the fast feet of the downhill journey.

In the past, it was hard to ignore a 'mountain'. But over the years I think I had gotten pretty good at it.

Now, I want to tackle that 'hill' or 'mountain' that gets in my way. Get it over with. Running has helped build my confidence to let me know that it can be done.

My next step in growth for running will be: *"Can I quiet my mind and do this without music?"*

Several years ago I was running a half marathon and my phone died at mile 6. My first thought was panic. *I can't run 7 miles without music!* Luckily, my heart stepped in and I told myself, "You can, and you will." It wasn't my most pleasant run, but it taught me that I can be alone with myself and be okay. I learned the same lesson on a long trail race where my playlist got out of whack, and only played easy listening music. I was scream face emoji, but ironically it turned out to be a relaxing run. I eventually turned the music down low and went with it.

Every day, I get more comfortable with just being with myself in quiet thought. Maybe introverts master this quickly, but this extreme extrovert crawled reluctantly to get to this place. I think I will always prefer chaos in some sort of way, or at least the presence of others, but I am progressing.

Small milestones: I can be driving in the car without music by myself. I can be in the house for days without turning on the television. I completed a 10K race without music, by choice. *Okay by force since music was prohibited, but I still chose to do the race!*

Through my time of injury, I even learned that I don't have to run to focus on resting and clearing my mind. I can simply sit on my back porch for an hour or two. This brings me to another thought—when I was young, I could sit on the front porch swing for hours. I could be by myself, or with others. It was a very natural thing.

I would just chill out. My favorite activity was to wear roller skates, and every few minutes I would hop off the swing and skate to the other side of the porch and back. No rhyme or reason. Now please tell me how I got to this place as an adult where I need to force myself to sit outside and do nothing, as if it were a chore, not a moment of leisure. Clearly, I need to invest in building a front porch and adding a swing—and buy a pair of roller skates!

I have a friend who loves to take long drives through the country in her car. She finds it peaceful and therapeutic. Indeed, there are many things we can do to just be with our own mind in thought. Other activities, however, are not quite the same for me as running because I also get a physical release. I've come to learn that I have options when running isn't available. The only yoga pose I do well is the corpse, which is a good one that allows me to just chill for 5 minutes at the end of the day.

I never thought I could be in this space. It took me a long time to get to a place where I could just let go of my need to be in control and allow my mind to be quiet.

Don't let me fool you, I still have moments of utter anxiety and panic that are totally unreasonable AND thoughts that concern ridiculous things. If I ever dared to say that I am a Zen spirit, my best friends would laugh out loud. *DAMNIT! I HAVE COME A LONG WAY, PEOPLE! PLEASE ACKNOWLEDGE!* Okay, me using all caps probably proves their point, but oh well!

Many days, I am faced with the epic battle between maintaining my inner yogi verses my type A, anxiety ridden, inner Kraken monster personality. I know that I can make things harder on myself, or easier on myself—it's all my choice. How I react to these small things is what makes a difference in my personal growth and happiness, both on the road running and in life.

Type A personality mind: "The line for the Port O Pots is too long. We will miss the start of the race!" OR "There's a traffic accident. I will never get the kids to school on time in all this mess!"

Me: "Namaste mind. Stay calm."

Type A personality mind: "The world is coming to an end, and I need you to react accordingly!"

Me: "It will be okay. So you start a little late. Just run your race." OR "It'll be okay. It's more important to teach them to react calmly to this situation than it is to freak out over something you have zero control over."

In the words of my friend Jaelithe: "It will. It won't. Who cares?" This was her advice to me on the anxiety that comes with working in sales. I've come to apply this wisdom to most everything, in a way that fits the situation. Sometimes it works to quiet the mind in angst, other times not so much.

Most of the time now, once I start running all that inner mind conversation dissipates as I become focused on the run. Soon, my mind goes where it needs to go.

This change in mindset has had a huge impact on my quality of life. It leaves me with much less anxiety, with a lighter heart and mind. I am not as bogged down, and I am more in tune with what my mind requires in order to perform at its best.

I can't always be running, though. I have to work and parent—a lot. Running is my main physical fix, but I also need mental maintenance between runs. We all do.

"The body benefits from movement, and the mind benefits from stillness."—Sakyong Mipham

This quote embodies so much of what I am devoted to in corporate wellness and ergonomics and in running. Getting people to pace themselves, give their minds a break, and keep their body in motion through the day. This is my passion and how I strive to live.

In life, our minds need breaks from all the everyday stimuli, which is just as important as resting the muscles, but this need is often ignored. Turning things off allows us to think more clearly, be creative, and achieve so many things.

For me, in life, turning off distractions has been the time I have been the most productive.

Business travel has always been a perfect time for me to think through ideas, and find solutions. Some of my best ideas have come to me on planes, running, walking, and even in the shower. Time away from the desk is good for me and the way that I am, and I don't think that we are all that different.

I love stories that include a picture of a scribbling on a napkin with the caption, "The idea that started it all." I feel like—that is my closing argument about being productive away from the desk—it can happen!

I realize that we all don't have jobs where this can happen, or where we can do what we do away from a computer. Regardless, all science points to the benefits of taking small breaks on the mind and physical body, which help us to be more productive either at our desks or away from them.

At work, I have constantly battled conventional American corporate mindset, which states that the best employees work until they drop, or the notion that more desk time equals more productivity. That battle has driven me to exhaustion. It is like running up a mountain that has no peak, no downhill respite.

Somewhere along the path, I realized that it is useless to talk with managers who have no ears for the topic. What has encouraged me to keep progressing on this climb are the managers who do seem to care. I see a small glimmer of hope in that maybe we can help workers who are chained to desks all day, with no reprieve. This hope drives me and others in the industry to keep the conversation going.

The US government mandates that hourly workers be given a 15 minute break for every 4 hours worked, in addition to meal breaks. There is a reason for this mandate, which is to protect the physical and mental health of workers. Salaried workers are in need of the same breaks, it is just up to each of them to schedule their own breaks if the job doesn't already have a system in place. Sadly, many don't or won't.

Mental wellness is so hard to quantify, to diagnose unlike something more physical like a carpal tunnel injury. Since mental wellness seems to be this 'enigma', it is easy for corporations to shrug it off. It has a huge impact on each person's quality of life, however, including their energy, stress, and anxiety.

None of this 'working more at the desk gives us more productivity' has proven to be true. What studies have revealed is that more screen time and time in a chair puts people at a higher risk for injury.

Now is where I have to calm my heart, because I desperately want to give everyone all the information there is on this subject. I will hold my passion back a bit though, and say this: "Please value yourself enough to know that not only do you deserve breaks, but you need them." Our minds and bodies were not designed to be shackled to a low-lit cubicle with no breaks.

To complete our jobs, we still need focused desk time, but we must not disregard the value of stepping away. Both physical activity and mental breaks help the brain work against aging. When we simply get up to get a glass of water or go to the restroom, we give ourselves a needed break.

Running has been shown to stimulate brain growth, increase cognitive function, and improve focus. It also promotes the release of endorphins, the feel-good hormones.[5]

Guess what? In this way, running is similar to meditation, which also improves brain development, memory, attention, and learning, as well as improved mood and wellbeing.[6]

The combo of the two activities can be quite beneficial for your health. Last month, I had a conversation with a corporate health manager about the positive effects of his program, which encourages employees to periodically step away from their desk.

Employees can choose between 15 minutes of group stretching or take a walk outside. What is really intriguing about his program is his high participation rates, and the high rate of employee satisfaction due to their ability to choose their preferred activity.

Programs like this make me super happy, because it shows hope that wellness programs can transcend the 'biggest loser' weight loss competitions to target the total body and mind connection.

In the meantime, while we wait—*OMG! IT'S TAKING SO LONG!!!*—for companies to put increased focus and importance on employees' mental health, it is up to each of us. We have the control every day to take our own small mental breaks from the world. Astonishingly, I have talked to people who have had bladder infections because they didn't want to get up to go to the restroom. I have talked to people who eat lunch in front of their computer screen—every day!

Research has shown what this does to you physically, and the mental part of this is not good either.

To help improve your mental wellness, you can do something as small as closing your eyes at your computer for two minutes every hour, and focus on your breathing. Another option is to integrate a 15-minute walk break into each four hours of work.

Several of my friends have spoken highly about the app *'Headspace'* for helping them calm themselves and practice their meditation. This app is something I am just now exploring for myself. I have read there are over 141 benefits of meditating, so I thought why not? Let me use just five, and I win.

> *"Quiet the mind, and the soul will speak"*
> —Ma Jaya Sati Bhagavati

WWGS: WHAT WOULD GRANDMA SAY?

She used to call me 'hurricane Annie'. There is a saying, "Sunshine mixed with a little hurricane." That is how she would describe me. I have always been high energy, with lots of activities going on.

I know—without a doubt—what she would say. She said it to me more than any other thing, other than *"Hold your shoulders back,"* and *"Would you like me to make you something to eat."*

She would say: "Come sit for a moment. Let's relax and watch _____ (choose one: the sunset, the fire, the water)."

Bless her heart, she was always trying to tame my hurricane spirit, just a little. Now, I think anytime I take time for a sunset or some peace, it is a nod to her. I listened. It took a while to get here, Grandma, but I am doing it.

WHAT DO YOU THINK ABOUT WHEN YOU RUN?

When I was pregnant with my first child, my sister Mary went with me on a work trip to Denmark. We carved out a couple of days to sightsee, including a visit to a sculpture park in Norway.

The lady giving the tour explained that regardless of cultural background or era, all humans can relate to the statues there. They resonate with everyone because they capture our basic humanity and portray senses of love, family, happiness, frustration, loss, and sadness, all through the most basic poses or simple gestures.

As a parent, I have thought back to these statues many times, particularly the little angry boy, Sinnataggen. I didn't realize at the time how I would come to fully understand this statue, once I had my son. It reminds me that all parents regardless of circumstance and location deal with some of the same basic joys and struggles of being a parent. It's a connection we all share.

Similarly, it seems that no matter how, why, or where in the world you run, we all have some very similar emotions and experiences. There are those times when you are just not feeling the run, you have pushed yourself to exhaustion or, on the contrary, that time when the run is so freeing that you can hardly put words to it.

There is that time that you break through a boundary, whether it's your first marathon or just making it around the block without stopping that makes you grin ear to ear. This is what I love about running!

When I watch running in the Olympics, I am in such awe of their pace and speed, but it is the sheer emotion of it all that gets me. On some small level, I feel like I can understand their feelings, even though I feel like I'm a chubby amateur runner who never competes in such a way. I do know what it's like to fulfill a dream, to do things I thought I could never do, to push myself, to run with my heart, or even to fall—that I understand.

I love hearing stories about learning moments, triumphs—anything with emotion. I also love knowing why people run and what is going on in their head.

With one broad stroke I feel I could answer: "Everything and nothing—with interruptions from an inner coach: keep going, slow down, speed up, you are half way!"

But there is so much more to know. Tell me about everything. I want to know what people are running to or are running from. I want to know where others find their strength, inspiration, and even amusement. We may be similar in the fact that we pull strength from our life for these things, but what exactly this strength is and what it looks like is each of ours to own.

Ann Hall, 45; Louisville, KY

When I am going up the toughest terrain I always think this is easy compared to what it is like to be a parent to a child on the autism spectrum. I channel the strength that I found in myself to handle our challenges and the strength that I see in my son. He amazes me with all he has overcome from such a young age.

"I could eat these hills all day because really, I just have to keep my head down and keep moving."

"Remember when my child wouldn't eat solid food for months because he had the fear of choking?"

"Remember when my child said he was stupid and didn't like himself?"

The complexities of deciding what to do next and the anxiety of when and how we would make it through those struggles—that was HARD! Imagine coming to a fork in a race with 10 paths to take, where only one gets you to the finish. The others lead to more hardships and traveling in the wrong directions, which will directly impact your child's wellbeing.

Comparatively, these hills I'm running up are nothing. I don't even have to think. I can just keep moving and let all my frustrations go. The path is clearly marked. It feels good not to have to make decisions on which way to go, but to simply go. I feel so strong from making it through the really difficult times in life that I can channel that emotion into any race. Likewise, I can take challenges from races, like running a half marathon in 45 mph winds, and apply this confidence right back to my life. This is what I think about when I run the most. Reflection on life and running—and thus one of the major inspirations for this book.

I think about my grandmother Edna. She left an abusive alcoholic husband in the 50s, when this was just not often done. She had the strength to make change. Someone once told me, "Nothing could stop your grandmother. She often walked out in the middle of farmland in heels and a skirt, and climbed over fences to talk to farmers about their insurance needs." When she retired, she was the president of a bank.

She had guts and determination stitched with a deep appreciation of everyday moments, like watching a sunset. I still think about how when she was dying she told my cousin, "Make your life count." I wonder if I am doing that, how I can become better, and what she would say about the things going on in my life right now. Sometimes, I feel as though I am talking to her when I run.

I think about my mother, who with an alcoholic and abusive father, by all statistics should be a substance abuser herself. She beat the odds, broke the chain of substance abuse that ran in my grandfather's family and gave my sisters and I a better childhood than she was able to have for herself.

She often tells me that she is proud of how strong I am to run and train. I think about how she is much stronger than I could ever be. I am proud of how she puts herself out in the world to try new things. I laugh about all her antics, including the time she decided to be a clown or collect fur skins to have their spirits cleansed by Native American Indians. I wish she would be less critical about herself … then I remember that I should be less critical about myself, as well.

I think of my daughter at age 6 wanting to run cross country. That little body with two blonde pig tails enduring the challenges of running in order to be with friends and earn a Popsicle. I think of how proud I am of her.

I think about the fights I have had with my sisters. Of course I feel they are being totally unreasonable, and that I am the one who is right. However, I also reflect on how lucky I am to have these two souls who totally get me—good and bad—to share this life journey with.

I think about how my aunt died and that maybe it was a blessing the way things happened so quick, even though we didn't have the opportunity to say a proper goodbye. I think about the exact tone of shock and joy that she would have in her voice if she saw me doing these long races. I miss her.

I think of my generous and kind Dad, and all his words of wisdom and stories. It is hard to live up to the kind of person he is, and my granny was. I think of her, too. It's been so long since she passed that I try to hear her voice and feel her hug so that I don't forget. She was born in 1902 and passed away at age 97. During one run, I found myself laughing, thinking about how she started showing up to water aerobics in a wet suit at age 94. If she had the guts to wear one so can I!

The last couple of weeks, my thoughts have been with my friend Susan. A rabbit appeared in my front yard that is mostly white with grey spots, not the average yard rabbit for my area. My friend Susan LOVED rabbits and had a pet bunny who hopped freely around her house. I wonder if she sent it to me.

She called and left a message on my work voicemail on a Thursday. I walked into the office on Monday and found out that she had taken her life over the weekend. That was 9 years ago.

I have been running to find forgiveness and to find closure for not returning that call right away. I realize that I may never get to the place of internal peace on this, but I feel I am getting closer. I know she wouldn't want me to feel bad, but I do because I think she really needed me or wanted to say goodbye.

It may be weeks that I go without thinking any of these thoughts, but give me something that challenges me to my core and my thoughts go right back to my family and friends.

I promise that I think about lighter things, too! On my better days, I think about everything good and just enjoy the scenery around me. I still practice finding one good takeaway or moment from every run. I try to imagine a time that I was running my strongest or felt my best, and go right back to that moment.

Cherokee Park remains my church. If I can run there once a week and reflect both on the past week and the week coming up, then I find myself much more centered and at peace.

Perhaps I think a little too deeply on my runs. My friend Chris thinks about things at work, and Jack Taunton was laser focused on trying to break 2:20 in a marathon. I have one friend who does math in their head during races and another who sets their sites on a person. Once they catch that person they eye the next person, and so on. The entire race is spent playing cat and mouse with people they don't even know.

One 10K race, a man with a tiny dog passed me. The man beside me was joking about the horror of being outran by this tiny creature with 4 inch legs. "Look at him and his smug elitist attitude. He probably can't wait to shit-up the course." At mile 5 I spotted the dog again. I knew how crazy it would be to get competitive with this little pup, but sorry—"Not beating me today my little four-legged friend!" I ran so hard to catch and pass him. That was a quiet victory on the outside, but on the inside I was totally elated.

Jaclyn, 35; Salem, MA
It depends on the day. Today I may think about what I need to get done for the week. Tomorrow, it may be something I said in a

conversation that I should have worded differently, and now I'm worried about how it came out. Sometimes I talk through something that is bothering me.

Other times I think about how much longer I have to run, and hate every minute of what I'm doing. When I start to get really negative, I try to think about how I have the ability to run and that there are people out in the world who cannot run, or do not have the ability to run. It helps me put into perspective that someone somewhere wishes they could be running, and that I'm the one outside running—and complaining about it. This thought really gets me to refocus and appreciate what I'm doing.

Krishna, 33; Holland, MI

At first, I think about the agony of running. I can then become distracted thinking about my playlist, the weather, my route, or my goals for the run. When I get deeper into the run, I focus on what I'm thankful for, my next steps in my professional or personal life, the run itself, or the environment around me. In the last part of the run, my mind is usually occupied with finishing the run and what that will look like.

Lucy, 54; Louisville, KY

Often, I utilize this time in nature to spend time with God. I thank God for my life and the gift of running and the people in my life.

Other times, I problem solve. I assess whether I feel like I'm 'on', or not … am I improving, or not.

On long runs, I find myself thinking of what a great breakfast I'm going to eat when my run is complete, and I wonder if I have time for a nap later that day.

Mike, 36; Dayton, OH

I don't run with music because I like to listen. I spend a lot of time reflecting on my journey in overcoming depression, losing weight, and more recently, dealing with divorce. It is a chance to think of all that I am grateful for now, and everything that is positive in my life.

Being a policeman can be stressful, so it is also an opportunity for me to clear my head and release all that stress from work.

Sarah, 45; Portland, OR

Mostly, I try to focus on how I'm feeling, both physically and mentally. I also try to focus on my breathing. Sometimes, I even meditate. If I'm on a path I'm familiar with, then I can slow down my pace, drop my arms a bit, and nearly close my eyes to focus on breathing deeply. If it's a straight path, I can close my eyes for a few seconds at a time. I did this in my first half marathon, and it felt so good that I now do it at times when I really need to zone out. I need to do it more.

Then there are times when I think about something that is bothering me. I always run hard and feel better after that.

Thomas, 48; Lexington, KY

When I run, I feel free. I have no worries. I know I am going to go out and run 13 miles for this race and I have two hours that I don't have to worry about anything.

I am a middle-of-the-pack guy. I set benchmarks for myself and try to stay within my training. My main focus though is to have fun and talk with people. You start the run and you end up running next to people. Some people leave you and some people join you. You have conversations. You may have a race t-shirt that sparks a conversation. I go out there and talk to people. Sometimes, people come up to you after the race and say, "You were a good pacer. I stuck to you for the race." That brings me joy.

I envision myself finishing the race. Even on my training days, which can be tough, I think about what it will look like to finish the race I have coming up. When I first started running, I could barely finish two miles. I couldn't even imagine myself completing a marathon. As I progressed and got closer to my initial goals, and then had to do long training runs of 15 or 18 miles, all I would see was myself crossing that marathon finish line.

VALUE *fit.* FORM. *and* FUEL

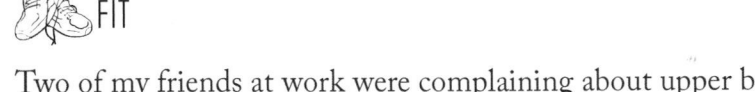FIT

Two of my friends at work were complaining about upper back and neck pain while they worked.

It actually pained me to watch the first person work. He was using progressive glasses to work on the computer, so he had his head tilted and strained backwards to see the screen clearly. His seat was so high that his feet were dangling off the ground. He allowed me to make some simple tweaks to his equipment and positioning.

As usual, changing the position of the equipment was simple … changing the behavior of the person was as easy as putting a square peg in a round hole.

He was less than enthusiastic to change, because clearly his pain was caused from the one day he spent bowling each week and NOT the incredibly awkward posture he sat and worked in for nearly 8 hours every weekday.

My plan was to keep stopping back by and making incremental changes until he got to a place of comfort. It does feel different to change the way you are used to working, even if that change is for the better.

When I visited the second friend, I asked him, "How did your workstation get set up this way?" He admitted he tinkered with the initial setup to make it his own. Basically, he created an ergonomic shit storm full of awkward postures, twisting, extended reach, and contact stress. He had been doing yoga and sleeping on the floor at home to try and correct his problems/pain.

He ALSO was less than enthusiastic to change the setup to eliminate the risk factors for injury, which he had created for himself.

In my experience, this is very common in the workplace. Workers treat their symptoms with chiropractic visits and massage, but don't address the root cause. If you turn a blind eye to the cause of your symptoms, you are bound to see recurrences.

My second friend is a runner and cyclist, so I had these thoughts for him: "Would you allow someone to extend your handle bars two inches farther away from you?" "Would you enjoy biking with your whole body facing straight forward, but your head cranked to look up and to the left the whole time?" "What would you do if the seat was hitting you in the wrong place?" and "What if the seat was too high?"

The answer for each of these questions, of course, is to go have the bike fit to you. Road bike riding is innately uncomfortable, so cyclists look for even the smallest ways to improve comfort and reduce muscle fatigue. I would say sitting at a desk for long hours, while staring at a computer and typing, is also innately uncomfortable. Our bodies weren't designed to be in static postures. They function best when they are in a nice neutral position, free of strain.

Even the most novice runner puts a high value on fit. The right style and fit of a shoe makes a huge difference in the quality of our runs, especially as we age. Get a shoe too tight and you might get blisters or lose a toenail. You might think a shoe feels fantastic and then out of the blue, you start having shin splints or hip pain. Runners look at things like the cushion, stability, width of toe box, and drop.

The quest for a perfect running shoe is like the hunt for a white cat in a snowstorm. Once you find a good shoe that works for you, you covet it like it was a family heirloom. I myself have hoarded 4 boxes of the same exact shoe under my bed. When I finally went through the last pair and found out they didn't make that shoe anymore, it was like someone telling me to go back to the starting line when I was at mile 10 of 13.1 mile race.

The point is, fit matters and it matters a lot, both in life and running. It has a huge impact on your comfort and performance. Your fit is individual to you and your body dimensions. No one person is average on all their body dimensions.

This is why it sometimes feels like you have to have a degree in rocket science to figure out all the adjustment levers on an office chair. To truly fit a person correctly in a chair, we look at things including distance from knee to bottom of shoe sole (feet should be flat on the floor), distance from buttock to knee (seat pan), distance from shoulder to elbow (arm rest height), and width of lower body (how wide does the seat need to be). Now, depending on what kind of support is needed, these adjustments can get even more complex. You get the idea, however, that many people could improve their everyday comfort at work just by taking ten minutes to learn how to properly adjust their chair, monitor, and/or workstation to fit them.

FORM

My grandmother told me every week of my young adult life, "Hold your shoulders back!" I can't say that this advice was ever met with the warmest of receptions. I would pull my shoulders back for a second to appease her, roll my eyes, and then go right back to my normal turtle stance.

As I have aged, I have seen pictures and thought, *"I really need to work on my posture!"* When I saw articles that would say, "Lose 10 pounds, just by standing up straight," I would think, *"Easy way to get results without work."* Except it actually was work. I never stuck with anything I initiated long enough to make the change. Although I did perfect holding my shoulders back when I looked into a mirror. This gave the great illusion that my posture 'problem' didn't exist.

Several years ago I was introduced to Romina Ghassemi, a chiropractor out of California who was educating the ergonomic community and workforce on posture. Listening to her was an eye-opening realization that indeed Grandma had been right—posture matters. It is our foundation.

Sitting like a turtle at your computer all day will hinder your performance, and will also start to stick with you. It is hard to be a turtle during the day while at work and have a super hero stance at night. After years of poor posture, it will start to follow you home. Much better to have the super hero stance influence you, than have the turtle take over.

As eye-opening as all this talk was, the tipping point on improving my own posture didn't come until I read an article that talked about how posture affects running performance.

Basically, the body works more efficiently with the shoulders lifted up and back. It opens up the chest area, which allows for improved breathing from the lungs. To achieve this posture requires strengthening your core and upper body. This posture serves people well athletically, as well as in their general life. A strong core and body is also a fundamental way to prevent injury as we age.

I visualized myself running in a power stride at top speeds while passing people on my way to the finish line and I was sold.

I started wearing one of Romina's Bax-U posture straps, and I turned to yoga for assistance. I was seeking the benefits of a strengthened core, stretching my tight and overworked muscles, and improving my flexibility. All of this led me to feel better, helped prevent injury, and yes—allowed me to run faster.

My more intense focus on core strength was brought about after I read a book for work, based on research from NASA regarding the role of movement in the physical healing of the body.

The study drew an interesting comparison between astronauts and those that led a more sedentary lifestyle. Super-fit astronauts go into space and rapidly become less healthy by living without gravity. Their muscles start to atrophy from not working against gravity and not being able to do weight-bearing activities. Those who are bedridden or are sedentary in general have very similar ailments, though at a different intensity level.

The good news is that when the astronauts return from space, they can repair their deteriorated health simply by returning to an active life on Earth. This lesson can be applied to the rest of us, those not doing space travel. If you have a sedentary lifestyle, you can restore your health by being more active. Gravity pulls on your body from head to toe, so its maximum effect is felt when you are standing. The more your body is working against gravity, the better your chances are of staying active and in good health.

Form in running doesn't end at posture and core, though. There is so much more.

My friend Jaclyn Norberg Morrissette (PhD, ATC), who besides being a wonderful runner, is an Assistant Professor and the Clinical Education Coordinator at the Athletic Training Program at Salem State University.

I thought I would pick her brain on the subject of form. It's like my Dad always said: "You don't have to know everything. You just have to know the right people to ask!" Besides reading her dissertation on race walking, I have observed her in action during our relay runs.

She can look at runner out in the horizon and say, "Oh, here comes Tammy." Everyone else looks at each other like, "Yeah right, how can you tell from that far away?" And every time she nails it. She can identify people from long distances just based on their gait. I don't know how many superpowers she has, but this is one of them! I think she must get a kick out of it when the rest of us can finally make out the person and say, "Damn! She's right again."

 THE JACLYN (J) AND ANN (A) INTERVIEW ON FORM:

A: What do you want people to know about kinesiology and running?
J: Kinesiology (the study of human movement) plays an important role in all aspects of life, especially running. Running requires coordinated movements of the entire body to occur and be efficient. How much arm swing, how long your stride, how quick your cadence, and the joint range of motion are all factors that can affect the running motion and ultimately your running performance. If you are unsure as to whether your form and movements are efficient, have someone take a video of you running either outside or on a treadmill. Once you see how you move, you can make adjustments necessary to better your running efficiency.

A: How does good and bad form effect running, respectively?
J: A runner with good form looks like they move effortlessly. They have equal strides, a smooth cadence, are light on their feet, and have a decent gap between their knees while running. Shoulders are relaxed with the elbows bent at hip level and move contrarily to the legs to help transfer force from the upper body to the lower body to make the entire running movement very efficient. Depending on the person and the distance, foot strikes will either be rearfoot or midfoot for longer distances, and midfoot or forefoot during shorter distances or sprints.

Bad form is pretty easy to detect after looking at someone with good form. Most runners, especially females, have weak hips, which will cause their knees to angle towards each other, also known as a valgus force. This force puts excessive stress on the knees, which can lead to injuries such as patellofemoral pain syndrome and IT band friction syndrome. Strengthening the muscles of the hip, especially the gluteus medius muscle, is a way to decrease this problem. The gluteus medius muscle is a muscle that helps stabilize the pelvis during running. Unfortunately, the way to strengthen that is through hip abduction (moving your legs away from each other laterally, like the leg portion of a jumping jack), which is not a motion that occurs during running. When this muscle is strong, it is able to stabilize the pelvis better and decrease the amount of valgus stress that occurs at the knees. Other indicators of bad form include loud foot strikes, regardless of where on their foot they land, strides and cadence that are not equal, shoulders that are elevated closer to the ears, and having a minimal arm swing.

A: Is it ever too late to improve your form?
J: I believe it is never too late. If someone needs to work on their form to obtain better performance, having their gait analyzed by a professional is the first place to start. If you do not know what is 'wrong', you will never be able to fix the problems. As a clinician, for individuals who are more recreational runners, incorporating a strength program is a good start in improving form. Videotaping your running can help you identify what issues you have with your form and allow you to make the adjustments necessary to better your form.

A: How can this make me, ahem ... I mean the readers, run faster?
J: The first thing I would ask you, I mean the readers, is whether they know what their weaknesses are in terms of their running form. If they do not know, having their gait analyzed is a good

place to start. This can be done in a biomechanics gait lab or at a running store if there is a certified biomechanist or exercise physiologist on staff. Once you know the problems, you can begin making the adjustments necessary to improve your form.

A: How does this kinesiology work for or against us in life outside of running?
J: Outside of running, kinesiology is important in all day-to-day activities. The foundation of all kinesiology is muscle movement. How your muscles move and how much force they can produce will determine how well all movements of life occur. When a muscle does not function properly, whether it is from weakness, tightness, or other neuromuscular issue, movements the muscle contributes to will not be complete or efficient. Maintaining strength, stretching/foam rolling, and cross training can help muscles function optimally. If the muscle works well, movements will be more efficient, regardless of what you are doing.

FUEL

As if working on fit and form wasn't enough work, I realized that I finally had to face the demon of nutrition if I wanted to improve my running. To come clean, I have been on and off 'diets' since my youth. During this time, I learned a thing or two about how to lose weight … and even more about how to gain it!

My real awakening didn't come until this year, when my running performance started to deteriorate and I also wanted to start doing triathlons. I was talking to my running friend Thomas Crisp. When I asked him what his biggest challenge in running has been, he replied, "Figuring out my nutrition needs." I had to pause to think, "So, people really pay attention to this nutrition thing, if they want to optimize performance?" Hmmm, maybe this will make me run faster.

I have spent a great deal of time over the years strategizing about how I can eat more and either lose weight or—at least—not gain weight. My strategy always brought me back to the same conclusion: build muscle and eat more non-starchy vegetables. The vegetables help to fill you up, and your body burns more calories digesting them than many times the calorie content of the food (thermic effect of food).

This year, I looked at nutrition in a whole different way. I focused on food as a fuel, not just something for enjoyment or health. I realized that I had been eating way too few calories to fuel my activities, plus I had eliminated many carbs. This made me feel sluggish in the long distance races. I had not even thought about refueling during or immediately after a race at that point. Why would I consume calories when I was trying to lose weight? The answer I found is: you can't increase performance and endurance while you are depriving yourself.

These days, there are so many options when it comes to different diets, and even more opinions. In the end, I decided to try tracking my macros. Basically, I used my weight and the number of minutes I work out each day to calculate the ratio of how many carbohydrates, proteins, and fats I could eat each day. I went from eating around 1300/1500 calories a day to 1900—AND I lost weight!

What I found is that by tracking and recording my intake, I helped stabilize my eating patterns. Some days I might only eat 900 calories because I tend to lose my appetite after doing heavy exercise. Other days, I would consume too many. Some days it would be mostly carbs and other days mostly protein.

Eating a diet based on a balanced amount of macros really helped me improve my energy levels. The benefit of this carried over into my general life. I now try to eat for what energy I need to sustain me. Even when I am doing recovery with much less activity, I stick to this way of eating about 80% of the time. The other 20% I am a woman in my mid 40s … with raging hormones, and so anything goes!

People will spend so much money on the right shoes, bike seats, gait analyses, fit tests, nutrition drinks, and supplements to enhance their sports performance. In life, many spend hours a day with bad posture in poorly fitted workstations and poor nutrition. They also aren't properly hydrated. Think of what minor tweaks in lifestyle could do to improve their overall life performance.

WWGS: WHAT WOULD GRANDMA SAY?

For starters, I think she would have totally loved this quote regarding posture: "Chin up princess, or the crown slips."

As for what she would say to me, it's easy: "Ann Wilson! Eat your vegetables. Hold your shoulders back. Go get yourself a good solid pair of shoes. Don't skimp on a mattress. A good night's sleep is important!"

Let me tell you, there is much more to the list. Grandma gave me a lot of unrequested advice. Who knew at the time she was right, except her. She talked about teeth cleanings and applying sunblock. She also always told me to wear good underwear. I don't think that applies to this chapter, but somehow I think she would throw it in here. Somehow, I think for her generation, the condition of one's underwear is a direct reflection on how well they have been parented. I don't really know what she would say if she found out that most runners don't wear underwear on their runs! I really wish she was around so I could deliver this news and see her reaction. I always loved to push her buttons—giant redhead reaction! Lol!

Of course, what I would really like to do most of all is give her a giant bear hug and let her know that she was right about so many things. I think she would get so much satisfaction and joy from knowing that I now think she was right. I'm holding my shoulders back grandma, *sometimes*. ;)

PEOPLE *first.*

My 7-year-old son Jack and I were walking in our neighborhood. He spotted his friend Parker and started bolting over to where he was. Parker was running up a small embankment beside a large drainage pipe that runs through several of our neighbors' backyards.

He dashed across the street and down the embankment on the other side. He had just gotten a new puppy and it had gotten away from him. The dog was streaking in and out of the pipe dragging the leash behind him. Jack started chasing the dog, too.

Mass chaos—two young boys, chasing one loose puppy. Cue angry neighbor. Here he marched, like Mr. Wilson himself had stepped straight out of a *Dennis the Menace* cartoon. "What are you doing?! Get off my grass!"

He made eye contact with me. "How can you just let those boys run loose like this? We just planted grass seed and the boys are going to ruin it!" He continued to yell at me and the boys as we scrambled to contain the dog.

I was just waiting for a rabid raccoon to jump out of the drainage pipe and join this little chaos party. Instead, cue his angry wife. She wasn't going to miss a chance to put her two cents into this mess. What a horrible, horrible parent I am—or so they said! I had never even met them before this day.

We finally got the dog under control and Parker immediately started to run home. I apologized to the couple and let them know that I didn't appreciate the way they were yelling at the kids.

As we walked away, my son started crying. He was worried that the man would come shoot him. I assured him that that wouldn't happen. For two weeks, my son was scared to go to sleep. It was months before he would walk down that street. Sounds extreme, but my son is on the autistic spectrum and has anxiety disorder. Little things can easily become big things.

I was talking to my Dad about this incident, mostly because of my son, and he said, "This is a man who put the value of a bag of grass seed above the value of his relationship with his neighbors. It is good to always remember to put people first." As much as I regret that this incident happened, it has been one of the great lessons in my life—put people first.

This tenet has served me well in life. When I feel the urge to get angry about something, I quickly assess—is this petty? Will this damage the relationship? Can I just let it go? It often boils down to what is more important, the item/situation/being right, or the person. I always tend to come back to the person.

In this way, I thought I had truly matured and evolved, then I started running. Here is where I tell you that for everything running has given me good, I have had times where I have considered discarding all of my humanity and life lessons to get a better time running. For a while, I took a step backwards in my personal evolution and developed an inner asshole.

Not just any asshole either, a giant asshole of epic proportions, that lived inside someone who on the outside looks like the Wendy's girl.

I have had thoughts of extending my arm out and clotheslining the shit out of people who bother me. I have been frustrated that people who are running in large supportive packs take up way too much space. When people have shoved or knocked me over, pushed me into puddles, or acted rude, I have called them names in my head that would make a gangster blush.

Finally, one day I had to confront this inner asshole and shut her down. I had to tell her that if she didn't behave, at least a little, I was going to have to tattoo "People First" on my arm as a reminder to myself of how I should be acting. When did I become so angry and serious about running? It's a game. Running isn't supposed to give me a pass to leave good manners and behavior at home.

Case in point, during a work trip I took a pit stop to run the Houston Minute Maid 10K run. I was feeling particularly good and ready to run that day. I ran from the hotel to the race in the darkness of the early morning. I ran a little faster than I had planned because I didn't expect to see so many homeless people hunkered down on the sidewalks. This both disturbed and scared me.

When I got to the starting line I got focused quickly. Early on, I caught a good stride and was running strong. My inner asshole felt good passing lots of people on the first incline.

I started to think that I might be running one of my best times. The elation of achieving a personal best had me extra motivated to push harder. Inside, I was jumping up and down with excitement.

This wasn't the prettiest course. Picture lots of dilapidated houses, un-mowed lawns, and construction.

As I pulled away from packs in the crowd to find a running spot that had a little more elbow room, I happened to see something out of my side eye. I turned to look closer, and in a blur the people were gone.

It looked like someone came up from behind a person standing outside in the construction zone, and with one swoop wrapped their arm around their neck and pulled them behind the hanging tarps.

Now, given that I have a big imagination and anxiety disorder, plus I watch a little too much *Law and Order*—I started to immediately unravel the worst case scenario in my head. A lady police officer was abducted by a murderer. I began to argue with myself.

Me: "You are imaging the worst. It was probably nothing. Don't create drama." Also Me: "… but what if it was something bad?"

I was still unsure of exactly what I had seen, or if I had seen anything at all. I passed so quickly and it was a blur.

Me: "You need to find one of the policemen on the route, and report this. Someone could be getting hurt."

Inner Asshole: "You didn't see anything. You are running the best race of your life. You are going to mess up your time."

Me: "What a horrible person you have become. You know the right thing to do. Remember your Dad—People First. Even it was only a 1% chance someone could be hurt, you go to help."

I spotted a police lady alongside the course and made my way over to her. I told her it was probably nothing, but it looked like someone pulled someone from behind into the tarped construction area. She asked me a couple of questions and said she would look into it.

I still had 3 miles to go. I returned to running and to talking to myself.

Me: "I can't even believe you would consider not reporting something because you didn't want to affect your time. Dad would be so disappointed."

Inner Asshole: "It is probably nothing and everyone will think you are crazy."

Me: "Still, better to be safe than sorry. You are a giant asshole and are taking running way too seriously. This is life. People and life always come first. You can never do this again. People before your race—not sometimes, all times!"

I couldn't stop worrying after the race so I went on a hunt for the police lady. She told me that what I saw was two construction workers playing around. One happened to be wearing the same fluorescent vests as the race security patrol. It was nothing. I was relieved, but still mad at myself.

On the walk back to the hotel I came up with WWIDL— *What would I do living?* And WWIDR—*What would I do running?* I decided that if I ever needed to decide something quickly in a race, I would have to ask myself what would I do in life, and that is exactly the answer for what I should do in race.

I can't tell you how many times I whisper "People first" in my head while I run. There are so many things to inspire you on a run, so many positive takeaways. I would be doing myself a great injustice to let that inner asshole control my experience. She is locked away now. Every once in a while she escapes—*PMS gives her strength*—but I shove her butt back in that cage.

Ironically, one of the best things about running for me has been the people.

At a race in San Diego there was a young boy with hulk gloves on cheering people from the sidelines. Runners were going over and giving him fist bumps. I really regretted I didn't make time for that. When kids are giving high fives, I try to make my way over. It's part of the joy and experience of running AND I was missing it.

The majority of people who run are beautiful souls, and as my mother told me, "If you look for good in people, you will find it. If you look for bad in people, you will find that too." We are all complex and imperfect, but if we search for the good it is definitely out there in spades.

I have shed tears of joy for people who I don't even know, never spoken a word with, because they have moved me that much. I saw a mother who saw her teenage child running in with a little over a quarter of a mile to go to complete his first marathon. She was running beside him crying, "You've done this! You have run a marathon! I am so proud of you!" There I was on the sidewalk crying, too. I felt like someone was going to ask me, "Are you his aunt?" I would have to reply, "No, I am a complete stranger who obviously has no control of her emotions."

I gave a hug to my friend Lucy when she crossed the finish line of the Louisville Ironman. I was completely elated. I saw my friend Linda cross the finish line of her first marathon the year she turned 50. Yep, tears. I saw my friend Lydia cross the finish line of her first marathon with her three cute kids so excited to be running beside her. Again, tears.

Apparently, I am a giant cry baby. However, I am not the only one who feels this way and who has shed a tear or two. I'm in good company.

My friend Henry told me a story of how he met a new running friend, who had asked him to pace him on the last 40 miles of an upcoming 100 mile run. For 35 miles Henry held onto his new friend's pace, which for him was still a bit fast. He just couldn't hang on anymore. His friend was okay and ran on. Henry stopped and sat down five miles from the finish. His plan was to find a ride to the finish since he was a pacer and not a race participant.

While he was sitting at the aid station, he saw a man who was hobbling in for a quick stop. The man was so severely chaffed from his privates down along his thighs that he could barely walk. He refused to stop though. This was his first 100 mile race, and he had only 5 miles left. His family was waiting for him at the finish. He may have to hobble it, but he was going to finish.

Henry thought, *"If he can keep going, so can I."* He agreed to finish the journey with the man. They endured the last five miles together.

Henry got to watch him finish the race. At the finish, the gentleman was so appreciative of Henry's company and assistance. That feeling Henry said of helping someone, a stranger just hours before, complete a dream was so touching. Perhaps, maybe, just a little, he teared up.

I adore this community of people who have such a common love for running that I can connect with them on so many levels. My running friends have given me far more support than I could ever repay. They have seen me at my best and worst, and cheered me on no matter what. They have given me the courage to try new things and have instilled confidence in me. I mean really, it is hard to keep in check the appreciation I have for my running circle. It's too large to be contained.

In life, I sometimes think I need to be more aware of the people around me and the opportunities I have to connect with them. It is easy to show up and leave, back to the comfort zone of my house. I like to stay in my own lane, outside the business of others, but maybe this is too safe. Maybe I need to seek more community outside the running and triathlon groups. I definitely want that for my children.

I once worked with a life coach who told me she had a mission in life that drove the decisions she made. It was, "I want to make the people around me feel better about themselves." What a strong statement that is to make. I can't even remember what my mission was at the time because I thought, "Why can't I just have hers?" I mean, I was being a total copycat pants, but that's the mission I want to have to guide me through this life. It doesn't get any better than that, does it?

About three years later I had a run-in with someone at work. My opinion was he was being a bully to others in the company. During a meeting with just him, I decided I would say something. He said to me, "My job here at work is not to make friends. I don't need friends. What people think of me doesn't matter. My job is to make sure we have a world-class department."

Well okay, then! Somehow I thought I was being kind by reaching out to him, but the conversation ended up taking a turn for the worse. We exchanged lots of words. Mainly I said to him, "I am sorry that you feel this way, but the relationships that you have here at work do matter and should matter. If they don't, I don't think you are doing it right."

In the end we agreed to disagree. I actually do agree that we don't have to be friends with everyone. That may be impossible. However, since we spend so much time with the people at work it would be much nicer if we are at least friendly and respectful with each other.

Life is so much less complicated when I try to live by the motto:

"Be someone who makes everyone feel like someone."
—Kid President

Can I do this all the time? Obviously no. Sometimes I still lose my shit.

Just yesterday, I wanted to flip off a rude driver while I was going down the road. Luckily, however, my inner yogi contained the inner asshole before any damage could be done. Later that day I saw a meme that said, "This fucker is going to be the reason I go to prison," and I evil laughed. That meme did give my inner asshole a little satisfaction. Muhahaha!

I'm too high maintenance for prison, so I need to keep myself in line. I am really trying to contain that inner asshole so that would never happen. I would rather have a life of rainbows and unicorns; dark chocolate, manchego cheese and pinot noir; or running shoes and a killer playlist.

I do try to remember what Maya Angelou said, "I've learned that people will forget what you said, people will forget what you did, but people will never forget how you made them feel."

When Grandma moved to a new town at the age of 75, she created her own welcome wagon. She threw parties and invited people in the neighborhood.

She was never afraid to put herself out there to people. People did nice things for her because they knew she would do anything for them, with no expectations of anything in return. She had a love for people. She made being with people look easy. I am an extreme extrovert, much like her, but I am much more awkward. I don't always find being outgoing to be easy.

WWGS: WHAT WOULD GRANDMA SAY?

Grandma would tell me what she always told me, "Get out there and have fun. Be a good friend." She would probably wonder why I would even have to think about putting people first in sports. She would think that would be obvious.

Do you think she would have cared if she was DFL (dead fucking last) or DNF (did not finish) in a race? No. She would still have lots of fun talking to everyone, and would have a great story to tell about the police parade following her as she brought up the rear.

My friend Henry said that one of the reasons he really fell in love with running ultra races was the people experience. He would encounter a person on the course. They would meet as strangers, but by the time they finished the race, they knew so much about each other. He met one man out on the trails and they talked for six hours. Six hours! He almost sold me on doing an ultra from his tales … almost!

"It's the friends we meet along the way that help us appreciate the journey."

Imagine SUCCESS

Today, my run felt out of sync. I have had to take some time off from running, and my legs felt like lead.

I had to reach deep into my imagination. "I am running with fast feet downhill on a trail. I have caught the perfect stride running and the run feels smooth and effortless and in the zone. I am bolting strongly towards the finish line with an abundance of energy. My legs are light and springy."

Better yet is when I imagine that I am running with the Olympic marathon team. We are all striding along together in perfect unison. "Nice day for a five-minute mile." I will probably let the leader of the pack win today. No need to disappoint the whole country of Kenya.

Yep, I may not have perfected my pace, but I have perfected irrational thoughts!

The one thing I have learned is that irrational thoughts serve a very significant purpose, and they tend to become not so irrational after all. Research has shown that visualizing success, or a time when you have been successful, can enhance performance.

When I visited a research lab at Texas A&M, one of the professors introduced me to brain behavior assessments. I was so fascinated to learn about the mind-body connection, and specifically how powerful the art of visualization can be on outcomes. During our conversation, we discussed studies that confirmed that performance increases when visualization is combined with activity.

Watching yourself lifting weights and imagining your muscles getting stronger can bring about more benefits than simply just going through the motions. In fact, some studies have actually shown results for those who didn't do any activity at all, only imagined it!

Not to be an evil scientist, but it didn't take me long to realize that I wanted to harness this power to run stronger and faster.

Apparently, visualization programs the subconscious brain. "When our mind believes we've achieved something desirable, the brain experiences a release of dopamine. That not only motivates us, but can trigger the side of the brain that learns from repetition. Repetition, whether in real life or in your mind, can help performance, whether you're an athlete or an entrepreneur."[6]

Coaches have used visualization techniques for years to motivate and prepare their athletes for success. Showing them videos of their strong past performances before their next event sets the brain on a course for repeat success. Pumping players up with inspirational stories and telling them they are strong is such a common ritual, from elementary school sports up to the professional level.

This increase in performance is more than just the power of positive thinking. In the book, *"The Brain That Changes Itself"*, Dr. Doidge writes, "Brain scans show that in action and imagination, many of the same parts of the brain are activated. That is why visualizing can improve performance."[7]

Personally I think this statement is incredible—visualizing can improve performance.

Imagine running around a track covered in snow. The first time you run the path, it is the most difficult, each time after the initial path has been created it becomes more navigable and thus easier to run. "Everything your 'immaterial' mind imagines leaves material traces. Each thought alters the physical state of your brain synapses at a microscopic level."[7]

Simply put, each time you imagine doing something, like running a route, you carve a track in the snow. It alters the tendrils in your living brain.

Studies looking at chess players, musicians, and athletes have all concluded that practicing in your head using visualization is beneficial to your actual performance.

According to an article, in *Psychology Today*, brain studies "reveal that thoughts produce the same mental instructions as actions. Mental imagery impacts many cognitive processes in the brain: motor control, attention, perception, planning, and memory. So, [through visualization] the brain is getting trained for actual performance."[8]

"It's been found that mental practices can enhance motivation, increase confidence and self-efficacy, improve motor performance, prime your brain for success, and increase states of flow."[8]

A study entitled, *Mental Power To Muscle Power—Gaining Strength By Using The Mind*, concluded that the mental training they used enhanced "the cortical output signal, which drives muscles to a higher activation level and increases strength."[9] Using mental visualization produced results in line with performing the actual physical activity. Mental visualization combined with physical activity contributed to the greatest results.

There have been many times I have experienced this boost from visualization, but was not even aware that it was happening. Times when I caught a glimpse of myself running strong in a reflection have always given me a surge of energy.

I thought about a time I was watching a bike race on the gym TV while I was on a spin bike. I felt like I was riding right along with them, working more muscles when they went up the hills and gliding when they were going down the hill.

Then I thought about how my favorite spin class instructors paint a visual picture of the journey as we progress during the session. Is that why they turn the lights down low, to help with visualization? Even though we are all pinned down, I must admit I always ride harder when I am in a class. I feel like I am racing with others up and down hills to either keep up or get ahead.

After reading this research, I was still left wondering, "How can I harness this new 'secret power' to run faster? Farther?"

What I discovered was that every time I run and my legs feel sore or heavy, I can imagine my legs moving lightly and smoothly along. I visualize past times a run felt great. I imagine myself running alongside a herd of animals, like gazelles or elite runners, because they look so effortless.

I found new ways to survive the times when I had to run on a treadmill rather than outdoors. I simply choose one of my ritual outdoor routes and run the same distance on the treadmill.

In my head, I bring up the starting point and then mentally go through the route, visualizing my surroundings on the run. Not just my surroundings, but how good I feel at different points on that run. I imagine my muscles working strongly on the up hills. I use the same technique on the bike trainer.

Other times, I play dance videos on my iPad and imagine that I am dancing along with everyone as I run. I am one of the coordinated dancers up front, not one of the ones tucked in the back. That is how strong my imagination is ... I can picture myself actually having dance moves!

One of my guy friends used to always exercise to the *Eye of the Tiger*, the theme from *Rocky*. I'll admit I poked fun at this a couple hundred times, but in reality he was spot on. His songs empowered him and helped him push harder.

Years later, this is my favorite thing— visualization along with music. Music transports me back to a time and place. I can see it, but I swear I can feel that emotion to my core—and doing that while running—I'm going to need a moment. Life magic times ten!

One of my favorite songs is *Shake it Out* by Florence and the Machine. This was always a 'good' song, but then I had this unbelievable life moment while this song was playing. Now when I run to it, I totally transcend back to this moment.

I recently volunteered at the swim exit of IronMan Louisville. This is the point that athletes emerge from the water after a 2.4 mile swim down the Ohio River.

Now, the swim is exhilarating for some, but super stressful and challenging for others. I will also let you know, if you don't already, that there are hard cut-off times for each event in the race. If you don't meet the cut-off time, then you get a DNF (did not finish).

We, as volunteers, were both in the water and out on the steps waiting in great anticipation for the athletes to arrive. We basically have less than two hours to get all 2,500 athletes out of the water through four stair chutes. Once the first athletes start arriving, it gets overwhelmingly crazy. People happy on the stairs, people shoving on the stairs, high fives from strangers, and people that are not able to stand up and need to be carried out.

Chaos and beauty, and then it starts to get quiet. The crush of people gets less and less, and we start to nervously eye our watch-es. "How much more time do they have?"

We can see the remainder of the athletes scattered across the water. I remember my hands actually clenching when I was thinking, "Please, please make it before the cut off."

To the left, the sky had turned black. A storm was rolling in. To the right, athletes were fighting the water to make it to us. Cue the song, *Shake it Out*. You could almost hear them willing themselves to just reach the steps.

The other volunteers were waving their hands like crazy so the straggling swimmers could spot us. For some reason, for at least a minute or two, I felt frozen in admiration. They just looked so majestic out there swimming. Lone swimmers with determination and heart giving everything they had to make it in. I was witnessing such a beautiful contradiction between the serenity of the water and the fight of the race.

Some had seemingly gone off course. Two were together, and that was hard to figure out. The lady would stop swimming for a second, and the man would wait. Someone yelled out, "He is swimming her in." We didn't even know if they knew each other.

Seeing each one of these last swimmers emerge from the water just before the cut off was overwhelmingly emotional. The sky. The music. The energy from all the volunteers and athletes. It really was a beautiful and inspiring moment in time.

The next weekend, I ran a half marathon and listened to that song during my run. I could feel the perseverance of the last athletes, their hope. My run was so inspired to that song, I was still in awe of that moment.

I read some of the athlete stories from the IronMan Louisville race, and one gentleman talked about feeling alone on the run course at night after most of the spectators had long gone home. A man on a bike with a giant boom box appeared. He was playing the song they use in the IRONMAN videos—*Hall of Fame* by the Scripts. This song gave him energy and strength. I run to this song now, too, and somehow it empowers me while I run to think of all the things athletes go through in order to endure.

If you visualize positive thoughts and performances, times when you were inspired or feeling strong, then your brain leads you in that direction.

So wait, what if you visualize bad things? Logic tells us that the brain is going to steer in that direction, as well. Replaying past failures and mistakes, telling ourselves that we can't do things, makes things harder for us.

No wonder coaches never say, "You probably won't win, just get through it." They always paint a mental picture of success, as do the best athletes. Sports have been said to be 90% mental and 10% physical. This means attitude counts.

If you think you can't be a runner, you have already begun to sabotage yourself before you ever lace up a shoe.

I was in comparable aerobic strength before and after I started running. I thought my pace being off was what held me back, but maybe it was my mental attitude as well. I am notorious for telling myself I can't do things. Perhaps the fact that I really didn't think I could do it made me more apt to surrender early.

My elite cyclist friend gave me some advice. I felt that what he was telling me put a lot of pressure on me. I told him, "I am never going to be an elite athlete!" insinuating perhaps that all of this was too much for me. He replied, "With that attitude, you never will be." Hmmm ... that caused me to pause and think. "Ugh ... he was right!" Even though I am not trying to be an elite athlete, I am trying to get better, and why put ceilings on myself about what I can or cannot be?

When I am insecure about an upcoming event, I now re-member all the events that I have done that I never thought I would be able to do, but did. I draw on past successes. If I can run a course that is 13 miles of Kentucky rolling hills, otherwise known as mountains, then I can run a 13 mile flat course in the rain. I always imagine myself as being strong. I somehow evolved to be able do this as I gained more experience running. It certain-ly wasn't something I thought about doing. It just happened.

If visualization has been helping me all along in running/biking, and I can use my awareness to have it help me even more, how can visualization help me at work and home?

Like running, I was already using it, I just didn't know a lot about it.

For many years, when I would get anxious on a plane I would take deep breaths. I would imagine my grandmother seeing me pull up in the car and come out to greet me. I could almost feel her embrace. I would also visualize sitting in the kitchen with my other grandmother. I could see so many details, including the particular way she held her hand on the table and tapped it as we talked. I could also feel the squeeze of her hug.

The longer my grandmothers have been gone, the more detail I lose in the visual. This is why I now try to bring that vision to mind on every plane trip. I would be heartbroken to forget a hug from either of my grandmothers.

I started to integrate visualization into my everyday life. At the start of the morning I take a second to visualize what the day will look like. What will I get accomplished? How will that look and feel?

I have heard of people using vision boards, where they clip out pictures that represent their goals and dreams about where they want their life to be. It could be a picture of a house they are working to buy, or a project they want to complete.

We already know that writing things down makes them 42% more likely to happen.[10] What happens when you can see your goal?

I have long pictured this book as being completed. I never thought it wouldn't happen. I told as many people as possible about it to keep myself accountable. About 85% of the people I told gave me a look as if to say, "Okay, sure you will write a book and get it published. God bless your little naive heart." This never made me doubt myself, it just made me push farther, harder.

I remember while growing up my grandmother would tell me, "You can be anything you want to be." She had so many stories about how people would underestimate her because she was a woman, and she never let it set her back. She kept pushing forward in life and in business because she had to, and also because she knew she could.

All the stories she told me of the strong, smart, and capable women in our family made me feel like anything was possible with effort. My mom was equally as supportive, and always complimented my writing and studies, even when they didn't earn me a top grade.

Was this the foundation of my confidence at work? Years of being told I was capable. They never told me what to be, only that I could be anything I wanted to be.

My grandmother once encouraged me to be a singer. I told her that I could not sing. She said, "You don't know that, because you never tried." She really did think I could do anything.

She had me thinking—maybe I could be a singer? A week later, she set up a karaoke machine in her living room. I enthusiastically sang one song. Afterwards, she patted me on the back and said, "Okay, you were right. You shouldn't be a singer." As easily as the confidence came, it went.

Many people in this life have succeeded not from being the best, but from having the most heart. Someone believed in them and they in turn believed in themselves.

Remember the *Little Engine That Could?* Based on his size he would have been the least optimal candidate to pull that freight train up the massive hill, but he thought he could when others did not. He repeatedly told himself, "I think I can, I think I can," and then he did.

One of my friend's mom's used to leave her sticky notes with positive affirmations on the mirror every morning. They would say things like, "You can do anything you put your mind to."

As positive as my grandmother was, I can only think that if I told her that my chubby little behind was going to run 13 miles for fun, she would have really had a nice laugh. I have also joked with my family that when I run up the large hill where my grandmother used to live, I can almost see my grandmother's friends saying, "Is that Ann Wilson?" while spitting out their coffee in disbelief.

There is one thing I know, though. If she knew I was serious, she would have supported me 100%. When she said I could do something, I knew she believed it.

That in and of itself was so much more impactful on my life than I ever realized. Her memory is a constant reminder for me to stay positive and encouraging with my kids and those around me. There really is power in positive thinking, and unfortunately there is also power in negative thinking. Many people don't remember all the good, but they remember the bad. It sticks and creates self-doubt—if we let it.

When my dyslexic son struggles to read, if I tell him, "You can do it," I need to believe it myself. People can tell if you are sincere. I need to help my kids visualize success for themselves.

I am not saying that we all have to have an ego the size of Africa, only that what we visualize for ourselves impacts the way we feel about ourselves and how we perform. This is why I have to keep working to silence that inner 'sports mom from hell' that lives inside me. I need her to be kinder, less critical, and believe in me more.

Someone once shared a short story on encouragement and believing with me, one that I would love to share with you:

> There was a group of frogs hopping along when two fell into a deep hole. The group of frogs at the top looked down into the massive hole. Seeing no way out they told the two frogs that had fallen that there was no hope left for them.
>
> The two frogs ignored what the others were saying and gave their best efforts to try to jump out of the hole. The group at the top kept saying, "You will never make it out. Give up!"
>
> Eventually, one of the frogs listened to the group. He gave up and fell deeper into the hole and to his death.
>
> The other frog kept jumping as hard as he could, despite the continued discouragement of the group. The group kept frantically yelling, "Stop the pain and die." This, however, made him jump even harder, which enabled him to make it out of the hole.
>
> The group was astonished that he made it out, and asked him, "Did you not hear us?" The frog then explained that he was hard of hearing and that he thought they were encouraging him the entire time.

The moral of the story is that words can have a huge effect on our outcomes. These words could be from others, or they could be words from ourselves to ourselves. Think successful, be successful.

"She believed she could, so she did."

PIT STOP

WHAT IS YOUR MOST MEMORABLE RUN?

When you ask someone what their most memorable run is, you open a conversation that could go in any direction. It could be a race or a regular run. It could be a tale of accomplishment, personal discovery, fighting the odds, miserable weather, perfect weather, struggles, success, simplicity, complexity … or any combination thereof!

Just maybe, the answer will be different from the same person each time you ask. For some, it is without a doubt a single point in time, every time. During interviews, many times when I asked this question I was met with a blank stare. I think, not because there were no stories to share, but rather how to do you pick from such diverse and meaningful experiences.

Finally, I turned the question on myself, and I realized that I too became an opossum frozen in headlights. So many very special runs! It is like when someone asks you, "Who is your favorite child?" Don't put me in that position! I love them all the same, but different.

Each time I asked myself the question, however, my Las Vegas runs were in the mix, so I decided to commit. These are not my favorite runs (different question), but runs that have had a very significant impact on my attitude regarding life and running.

Ann Hall, 45; Louisville, KY

My first half marathon in Vegas was a night race down the strip with my sister. It was the perfect day weather wise, but by the time the race start came around, out of nowhere came cold, rain, and high winds. I was in the last starting corral, which meant I had over an hour wait. I curled into a ball and tried to will myself to be warm.

Fast forward, I ran strong, but those 45 mile per hour winds were so tough. It was not a race. It was a battle. I spent a lot of time talking to myself, trying desperately to find enough strength and confidence to keep going. I finished much like the way I started. Crossed the finish line and immediately found a place to again curl myself into a ball, to try to stay warm while I waited for my sister.

It wasn't the race I planned on, but it was the race I got. So many times after this race, when things would get difficult in a run, I would always think of the perseverance and strength I found inside me in order to get through that Vegas race. If I could physically endure that race, then all other races should be easy in comparison.

At least I thought that until I returned to Vegas with my sister the next year for my redemption race. Everything had been planned perfectly to make sure that this would be a great race, or so I thought.

When will I learn you can't control the race?! Stuff happens! I ate something that didn't sit well with me for breakfast, then I got so excited about getting to the race that I forgot to eat lunch and I didn't pack nutrition.

Right before the race began, at around 6 pm, my stomach cramps started. Mile two, I dropped my ear buds. As I tried to pull them up another runner stepped on them which ripped the earbud off of one side. Mile three, I drank some water and my cramps worsened. I kept pounding water because I didn't want to get dehydrated. From this point in the race until the very end, I threw up water every half a mile to a mile. To be clear … that is 10 miles of throwing up!

Mile six, my phone died and I was forced into my first ever long run without music. I am not sure why I kept going, especially with all the stomach discomfort, but I can only say that I never once thought about stopping, only getting to the end.

At the medical tent just past the finish line the doctor gave me Tums that stopped the cramping and made it possible for me to keep fluids down.

I wanted to have a perfect race, but instead I had gastritis and what I considered at the time to be a run from hell. Now, I would also like to tell you that I handled this situation gracefully … but I have to admit that my inner asshole was strong on the mile walk back to the hotel. Instead of commending myself for enduring, I was beating myself down for poor planning and performance.

I was in my head feeling sorry for myself, until out of nowhere someone called out to me. There was a younger gentleman dressed in military camouflage sitting in a wheelchair on the walkway. He locked eyes with me, "You are so beautiful!" he said. I blushed and smiled at him.

Embarrassed from the stares of others, I put my head down and continued to walk. I reached into my pockets. I had my hotel key and my dead phone. I had no money or food to give. As I continued to walk to my room, I thought about what an asshole I had been.

I was feeling sorry for myself for not having the perfect race. What kind of problem is that? I should be so lucky. Here is a gentleman who appears to be homeless and in need. He had a smile and offered to cheer up another soul, which happened to be me. It reminded me of the plaque on one of my favorite statues, which states, "I who have nothing bring." It is a statue of a young girl carrying a giant heart.

This last Vegas run gave me two things. It kicked my ass on the subject of perspective, which has been a positive thing. It also gave me another tough race that I could say, "If I endured those two tough races, I can get through this."

I am not quite bat shit crazy enough to tempt Mother Nature (or life) to give me more challenges. I just know I learned that I was tougher than I thought. So many times I have looked at a situation and thought, "I can't do that." Uh, yeah you can. If you are forced to run without music, you find out, yes you can do that. It may not be as enjoyable, but I have learned to stop boxing myself in by defining what I can and can't do.

If a race didn't go as I planned, I have to remember, "It did go as planned, just not MY plan." There is a distinct difference. In the past, my expectations of how a race should go have created considerable grief for myself. That was my own doing. The races went how I needed them to go for personal growth. I have perhaps learned the most about myself and from myself during those times when my race expectations went off-course.

I would not trade those memorable races for anything, because they are part of my journey. If all my races had been perfect and to plan, I don't think those magical races where things just fell into place would be so special.

I have decided that I have three types of races: races where I run well and easy (or at least comfortable), races that aren't so easy where I learn something, and races where shit really hits the fan and I am left with a good story to tell.

Jaclyn, 35; Salem, MA

My most memorable run is a tie between two runs. Both of them happened during 2017. The first was the Smuttynose Half Marathon, where I beat my best half marathon time by 8 minutes. It was the best race I've ever run, I'm not sure I will ever be able to beat it, and I'm totally fine with that.

The other was my first, and most likely only, marathon, the New York City Marathon. It was my most mentally challenging race, but I never felt the urge to give up. When the pain of the run diverted my focus, I thought about what I always think about when I'm mentally struggling: "There are people out there that want to run, but can't (for whatever reason, physically or mentally) and here I am running with no issues and complaining that I have 2 more miles to go. There is no excuse to not get this done. Just finish!"

Krishna, 33; Holland, MI

My first long continuous run (over one mile). I started from my friend's house in Maryland and we ran 6 miles together along the Potomac.

Lucy, 54; Louisville, KY

My most memorable run was the finish of the Boston Marathon in 1996. My youngest was 2. I had trained most days pushing her in a racing stroller for 6 mile runs.

In my high school running days, Kathrine Switzer had just gone under the radar, well sort of, to run the Boston Marathon. She had entered using her initials as women (at that time) were not allowed to enter. Her boyfriend had to body block officials from pulling her out of the race because it was felt women could not run a marathon. I remember my joy for this moment. If we can't, then let us try. If we fail, well, we'll just try again. And she didn't fail … she broke down a wall for women's distance running with style, joy, and victory.

Someone came up to me in the hall at school and said, "Lucy did you hear about Kathrine Switzer finishing the 26.2 mile Boston Marathon? Not even you would do that … right????"

I was overjoyed, and replied something to the effect of, "Yes, I will do that before our 20th class reunion."

I had some added challenges in my first marathon in 1995 and finished in a 3:52, and so did not qualify for Boston. By the grace of God though, I was one of 100 chosen by lottery to run Boston in 1996 (5 years before my 20th reunion).

The night before the race I had bursitis in my knees and was getting very nervous. My young children were jumping on the hotel beds enjoying their own adventure. I love to race, but I was really getting anxious.

> *"Sometimes reaching a dream is almost scarier than not reaching it … almost."* —Lucy Monin

Fear tends to make me frustrated with myself, until courage wins the day. So I was in awe as I entered the athlete's village and my gate to start the race. It was every runner's gold medal dream to be there (though for me I was still a bit haunted by the fact that I had missed qualifying … which will still haunt me until one day, God willing, I do it).

Anyhow, the crowd during the race was beyond awesome. I had made it to the top of Heart Break Hill when I heard my daughter yelling "Mom," so I ran back down it to hug her. Some college-aged girls were there and they yelled, "Wow, Mom is running the Boston Marathon! Way to go MOM!!!"

With renewed energy I ran back up to the top of the hill and onward. I faced the up and downs of Newton's Hills. When I turned the last corner 26 miles in, and saw the finish line it was a true mind, body, and soul experience of joy. It was something so pure that it is hard to put into words. I crossed that line with such joy in my heart. I was trusting God's plan for my life as we headed 2 miles away to a train station to go grab breakfast.

Sarah, 45; Portland, OR

Oh it is so hard to choose! I would have to call it a tie it between my first half, the Columbia Gorge half marathon, and the Detroit Free Press International Half Marathon. For the Columbia Gorge Half we had spectacular weather, which was unusual for late October. They bussed us up this massive hill to the starting line. I learned on the bus ride up that this was the first year they changed the course so we didn't have to run up the hill. I was so thankful for that. *That is when I learned I needed to start looking at elevation maps when I choose races, because unlike Ann, I am not fond of hills. I am trying to work on that.*

We still had quite a bit of the hill to climb at the start. On the way back, close to where we started, I was given a half a banana—which tasted like heaven to me! Ever since then, that's how I fuel during a long run; I wear a running belt with a banana stashed on the side. Very shortly after I finished that banana (around mile 9) I had a great long downhill run to the finish line. I looked over to the side and was able to see the finish line. I was so excited to finish. After crossing the finish line I called my Dad because he had done the Ironhorse Half Marathon in Kentucky that same morning. We compared our times and we realized that we were spot on, almost to the second! I finished one second faster than him. It was so encouraging to know that I was as good as my Dad, who had been running for 40 years at that time.

The Detroit International Half was so great because I had friends running the race with me, and my entire family was there, too. My Dad registered too late for the International Half, so he had to run the Detroit only race which started later. This meant that he was able to be there to see me start and finish. The race course took us over the Ambassador Bridge into Canada. We had to submit our passport numbers ahead of time and carry our passports with us during the race. I swore if they stopped me, I better get some very cool stamp in my passport! After crossing into Canada we ran along the waterfront for a few miles and then into the tunnel crossing back over to the US. My parents and daughter were there as I came out of the tunnel. My mom even handed me a banana. That was the first time my mom had been to one of my races. It was so great to have friends and family there, and to be able to run a race in another country.

Mike, 36; Dayton, OH

My most memorable race was IM Louisville in 2013. This is when that race was still held in August, so it was very hot. Being new to 140.6 mile races I still was in learning mode on things like nutrition and hydration. I had taped all sorts of food to my bike, but my nutrition for the race was still off. I didn't eat or drink anything, besides maybe a cup of water, after the 80 mile bike point. That was 30 miles of biking and a full marathon with no more nutrition. The only thing that got me through that run was my mind.

When I finally rounded that final corner, I immediately started crying. I couldn't stop thinking about how far I had come in my journey. I went from weighing 350 pounds and not wanting to live, to completing one of the hardest events in sports, and I had a new positive outlook on life! It was such a defining moment for me.

To make things so much better, I had a lot of friends and family who took the time and effort to drive to see me finish this race. They got to witness and share that moment with me on my journey. Louisville will always have a special place in my heart because of that race and day. In 2016, I left that race after finishing it for the second time saying, "My heart is in Louisville", and that holds true to this day. I will always go back there, it's one of the best and most fun venues on the Ironman Circuit.

CHALLENGE *yourself*

9

Peter, a long-time and dear friend, is often filled with the best and worst advice. He once told me that I should stop birth control pills if I wanted to have children in my 30s. He said it could take years to conceive. I stopped the pills in December and in February the doctor told me I was 7 weeks pregnant. Unbelievably, I went in to see the doctor because I was sure that I had cancer or some other horrible disease that was making me feel so bad, and got the surprise of a lifetime—there was a baby in my belly!

See? Peter gives the best and worst advice. I got my amazing son from his advice, but the part about taking so long to get pregnant ... uh, nope.

Anyway, I ran a half marathon with Peter this October that went through my favorite park. I felt good, well not just good, I felt great, inspired actually. I knew my daughter, sister, and nephew would be volunteering at a water stop. This would be the first time my daughter would ever see me run a race.

I ran that race with so much heart. I hadn't put any expectations on myself, other than to show up and run. The first half of the race I was running to my family. The second half of the race I was overflowing with the excitement from seeing them. At mile 12, I caught up to Peter and his daughter Lea. We all finished around the same time.

After the race, Peter told me, "You were running strong. You looked like you could have been running faster." He actually said it a couple of times. I spent several days thinking about what he said. I set a huge PR (personal record) for myself that race. It was the first time I ran a half-marathon with all my miles under a 10 minute pace. I had never even came close to that before, and I hadn't even tried to do it. It just happened. I ran a great comfortable race, but I knew Peter was right. Maybe I was capable of more. Maybe I wasn't challenging myself enough.

Sometimes, we need someone else to point out things like this to us. Given that it was Peter, I was about half sure he could be right.

I had a race coming up in Nashville, and I thought, "Let's try and break two hours, which is an overall pace of 9:10 MM." It seems a little unreasonable to make a PR and then try to break that PR by 8 minutes only three weeks later, but that is the type of dickhead stuff I do to myself sometimes. Peter never insinuated I should do something like that, just that I was capable of doing more, giving more.

What if, though, I simply put this maybe a 'bit too challenging goal' out into the universe by speaking it into words? What if, instead of putting pressure on myself, I just see if I can do much more than I thought I could do? I don't want to hurt myself, but I want to achieve something I never before thought possible. I decided to go for it. The goal was to, "Stretch the rubber band of what I can do, but not break it."

My final pace for that race was 9:13 MM by my watch. I just missed it, but I was filled with elation. It felt good to stretch myself towards a seemingly impossible goal, and then almost touch it. My inner asshole was a little mad that I just missed it, but I had to reason with myself. I did reach a goal that I never thought I could do.

I learned in running that I can start to nuzzle into my comfort zone and not even realize it. I do it in life too. I thought that I had been challenging myself by doing new things in running, yet somehow I still found a way to be a little risk averse. Can you be complacent and still run? Uh yeah, you know I have found a way to do this at times. I have dialed in my fair share of runs, and as they say 'sandbagged' what my pace would be when running in a group, just in case I wouldn't be feeling it.

Thanks to a friend who had confidence in me, I challenged myself in a new way. I subsequently made new more aggressive goals, and found that they were in fact reasonable, unlike other times, because I had been training all season.

I haven't really been that proud of myself for something in a long time. With this new realization, however, I had to acknowledge to myself how far I have come. I realized that sometimes I hold myself back because I set limitations for myself regarding what I can and cannot do, without even consciously recognizing it. I knew I could run, but I didn't know that I could be so much faster.

This year has been the strongest race season of my life, it almost makes me nervous because a big part of me thinks that I can never top what I have done this year. Yet I've thought the same thing pretty much every year I have ever run. As confident as I can be in some areas of my life, a part of me always thinks this about my running: "It's a flipping miracle you got to the place you are now. It won't last."

This year I was able to break limitations I had set for myself by competing in triathlons and getting new PRs. I was running on the treadmill one day, thinking about this and the reasons why I keep challenging myself. This was on my mind because I agreed to do my first marathon next year. All the running and races I've done, and I have still never completed a marathon. I just never wanted to run that far all at once. Until now.

Every time I ran a half marathon, I would arrive at the fork in the road that pointed towards either 13.1 or 26.2. I was so relieved to follow the 13.1. I have never looked at the other side and longed to be running more. Nope, I was ready to head home.

I'm not exactly sure what changed, except maybe I think that the 13.1 distance just isn't challenging me like it used to a couple of years ago. I didn't really have a deep conversation with myself on the subject. I just decided on impulse—much like I do with everything else—that I was going to do it. I then told my virtual friend Erica, who I met on a running board, about my decision to do it. We decided to do our first marathon together. *Maybe I invited myself a little if I really think back on it.* That was it. Done. Confirmed.

Sister: "You are flying to Texas to do your first marathon with someone you met online?"

Me: "When you phrase it like that it makes it sound weird, but yes, that's what I am doing."

Now, I haven't even started training for the marathon, but I am thinking about going ahead and signing up for a half Iron-Man. That is 70.3 miles of swimming, biking, and running.

So back to me on the treadmill this morning, why do I seek such great challenges? Doesn't regular life challenge me enough? I mean, this year personally has been one race that I can't wait to cross the finish line from and start fresh.

I started the year battling eye disease. I have a retina issue, which is something that glasses can't fix. My sight had gotten so distorted that there was a chance I might be visually impaired. Besides struggling to read, the lowest point was when I looked at my daughter's face and could not see it clearly. It wasn't as extreme as looking at a reflection in a funhouse mirror, but was along those lines.

I had just taken a new job, which I loved, and was well over halfway through writing this book. I felt like I could lose everything if I couldn't read. At one point, I didn't even know if I could keep my drivers' license. How was I going to get around with the kids?!

Talk about a long, stressful, and challenging road. Thank goodness medicine has come a long way since the last time I had this condition. Over the last 10 months they have been able to restore my sight to almost back to normal, minus the permanent damage from the last time I had a flare up.

I have had even more challenges this year with my divorce, children, work, etc. ... so why in the world am I putting myself through all these other challenges?

I don't have a clearly defined answer, but I can only think that it is because I need it. Monotony doesn't serve me well. Not just in sports, but in work and pretty much anything. I am always looking for a new focus, something interesting, and a challenge that I can work to achieve. It is when I am at my best. I'm also always looking to stretch the envelope of what I can do. It feels amazing to achieve something that you weren't entirely sure you could do!

The yin and yang of my personality are always at battle. I crave adventure, yet I am sometimes scared of it. This is where business risks seem easy, what's the worst that could happen? I mean I worry about having cardiac arrest on a running course, being abducted on a run, or being mauled by a bear on a trail. But in business, what is my real risk? I go for an account and don't get it? I try a new job and it doesn't work out? I find another one.

The other day at work someone asked me why I was trying to work with some of the biggest clients in the industry, insinuating that I could never get them. I guess I foolishly think that I always have the possibility of winning, if I at least try—I visualize success. I like being the underdog in a lot of situations. When no one expects that much from you, when you do win, you really win.

Again, how many of my friends thought I was really going to write this book?

Sister: "You're writing a book on running?"

Me: "When you phrase it like that, it makes it sound weird. But yes, that's what I am doing."

I have been talking to my imaginary friends through writing for years, so really it's not too far of a stretch. I mean I don't have an education in writing books. When it comes to running, I am a middle-of-the-pack amateur runner. So, this all totally makes sense and is reasonable—to me.

My friends seem to fixate on this: "What makes you qualified to take on this challenge? Are you not setting yourself up for failure?"

And I, in contrast, seem to fixate on this: "Why not?"

Runners are always trying to run faster, go farther, achieve a personal best, or cross over into a new sport. It really comes down to running your own race and finding ways to compete with what you think you can do and what you can actually do, as I see it anyways.

> *"The real purpose of running isn't to win a race, it's to test the limits of the human heart."*—Bill Bowerman

What if people challenged themselves like this more in life? It seems reasonable to go from being a 10K runner to running a marathon with training, but why are people so closed off about going from, let's say, writing a blog to writing a book?

The thing I have learned about me challenging myself the way that I do personally, is that I am okay falling. I don't see it as a failure, actually. I may beat the hell out of myself regarding the metrics in sports, but I also have a side of myself that doesn't care what others think. My battle is internal.

It is hard to win big, without learning from all the times you don't win big along the way. I see these challenges as a great exhilarating attempt at learning that may have success as a reward, but also maybe not. At least I get to enjoy my dream during the ride. I may also have a funny story to tell, based on the experience. I think I have gotten to this place in part through sports.

When my grandmother said, "Make your life count," I took that as a personal challenge. In essence, she gave me the permission to go for things in life. I don't intend to hold back and let silly things like having no experience in book writing and the fact that I am a mediocre runner hold me back from doing exactly what I want to do—write a book on running.

How else am I going to make my life count? I am still trying to figure out how to do that, though I am sure it is different for everyone. I just know whatever this looks like, I won't find it on my couch watching television or doing what I have always done, day after day.

"Life begins at the end of your comfort zone." This is on a magnet on my microwave. There is life in the comfort zone, but I think the statement refers to an entirely different type of life. This is 'roller coaster ride' life verses the 'motorized cars on the flat course' life. *All life has some roller coaster aspects, I am talking about everyday life.*

The roller coaster life is full of firsts, failed attempts, and the exhilaration of when something works, much like running. This is my interpretation anyway. I am sure my grandmother never ever had running in mind when she said to me to make my life count.

The one who falls and gets up is so much stronger than the one who never fell.

My grandmother kept journals of her life from childhood until she was too sick to write. That's 60 years of writing every day. Is that my next personal challenge? I hope I have the courage to even read those journals. She wanted me to read them and write her memoirs. *Please don't tell me they are too saucy, I won't be able to pick myself up off the floor.*

As you have probably guessed from my accounts of her—I loved her so dearly. Thinking of reading those journals makes the loss of her more real. I tried once. I am not ready to take on that challenge just yet. Soon.

My grandmother and I shared a love of writing, *my mother and daughter do, too.* I like sharing with others. I like collecting my thoughts on paper. I think this project would have delighted her. I also think she would be so pleased with me running. The only person more shocked than me that I run would have been her, but I think she could identify with how and why I run.

If I have to choose between a long boring flat course and a hilly course. I will choose the hilly. I like not being able to see what is coming up next. Surprise me, let's keep things interesting.

Running may be hard, but when compared to life, it is a great distraction for me. It keeps me healthy and makes me feel good about myself. Personally, I have proved to myself that I am stronger than I ever thought I could be.

Just like in life, when things start to get complacent, I need to find a new challenge to reignite my passion. After working the same job for 15 years, one day I just realized I was done. This wasn't some huge drama that people wanted to paint it out to be.

I was appreciative of my time at the company and my work family, but in my gut I knew that I would soon just be going through the motions if I stayed.

It was pretty darn scary to start over, but it was also so exhilarating. I had to scrap for about two years to carve a new place for myself, but when I found my place I felt super inspired and passionate again.

WWGS: WHAT WOULD GRANDMA SAY?
She would smile and say, "Have fun with life!"

WATCH *expectations* and *choose* HAPPINESS

10

"She believed she could, so she did." And sometimes she didn't, at least not yet. It wasn't her time.

I can't tell you how many days I woke up thinking, "Today is the day I am going to get a PR." I would enter a race with expectations at an all-time high, and then I was left feeling incredibly low if I didn't make it.

I find that there is this thin line between setting myself up for failure, overstepping my expectations, and allowing myself to grow by setting goals that challenge me.

Case in point, I really pumped myself up at the beginning of the year with all of that visualization research. If I can see it and believe it, then it can happen. Maybe I underestimated the part about having to work hard for things, too. Visualizing success is gold, but it is only part of the equation. All of these things work in unison.

Last summer I ran the Run Houston NASA Race. This was a note from my journal that day "I have been doing all this research and work with positive visualizations, why not apply it? Visualize success!"

In my head I was going over what a great race I would run. Right before the race started I could see the master runners group finishing and I was visualizing—I could do that!

About one mile into the race I had the realization, "Oh yeah, running is not easy, especially in Houston summer humidity!" I was trying to slow my initial pace down so that I could ease into a faster pace. My mind was shifting from, "I'm going to get a PR" to "I just need to survive."

Every time I would think about pushing just a little harder, I would look at the heart rate monitor on my watch. My heart rate was too high, so instead of speeding up I needed to slow down. Sometimes, our body doesn't cooperate with what our mind wants us to do.

For about 6 hours after the race, I went over every detail of what I did days before the race and during. I was so hyper critical of myself, evaluating every move to see what I did wrong. My inner asshole was being very unkind to me. I would never put that kind of scrutiny on someone else. I forgot to enjoy the moment and be proud that I finished the race. I got too caught up in the numbers, AGAIN!

In my mind, I totally tanked the race. My pace was more than my half marathon pace AND it was a totally flat course!!! I posted my thoughts online on a running group page. Specifically, after I briefly described my 'failure' I asked, "How do you cheer yourself up after a really bad race?"

Everyone was so positive and supportive. I started to snap out of my funk. I mean I ran 5 minutes slower than last year's time. Is that really such a tragedy?!

I guess my attitude about the race boiled down to the expectations I set for myself. Before the race I was visualizing myself winning. I had been running stronger in previous weeks, but I wasn't on any kind of training plan. I was definitely not acclimated to the humidity, so my expectations were totally unreasonable.

Success is not guaranteed every single time we do something. If it was, it probably wouldn't be so gratifying. Even when we plan, train, and do everything right, we need to expect the unexpected.

This running thing can be quite fickle. You can run the same course, even under the same conditions in the same month. One time you may kill it and the other time you will wish you were home doing taxes instead of running. This is part of the 'joys' of running.

I have learned that the sooner I can let the not so good runs go, the happier I will be. Better yet, if I can adjust my expectations right from the start, to be more flexible and positive, then I don't have those low moments in the first place.

It doesn't mean I still can't challenge myself, I just need to be realistic to know that it might take several attempts to get to the goal. I need to be open to this. As they say in IRONMAN, "Always earned, never given."

Edward De Bono, a psychologist and author says, "Unhappiness is best defined as the difference between our talents and our expectations."

I know I have struggled with expectations that I put on myself and others in my life, but in running I have gotten truly ridiculous. Even more ridiculous is how many times I have bonded with other runners about this. Apparently, I am not the only runner that gives themselves high expectations and then beats themselves up over not meeting them. One triathlete I talked to said he used to punish himself by making himself run again when he got home from a bad race, if he didn't meet his expected goal.

It took someone in one of my running groups over 5 years to finally break their PR for a 5K. I HOPE that for five years she didn't berate herself for not making it each time. Instead, I hope that that journey was one of determination, perseverance, and faith—AND that when she finally accomplished it, she was elated.

Expectations in life have been a considerable source of a lot of heartbreak for me. My favorite meme simply says this:

Six word story:

What hurt you?
My own expectations.

This is so true. Romantic relationships, family, work, friends … the expectations I put on myself, even for silly things like keeping a clean house. Please can we all redefine what a 'clean' house is when you have kids? My house will be clean when they are out living on their own. For now, it is clean enough. One day I am going to miss stepping on Legos and finding kid's underwear stuffed behind the toilet.

Probably the biggest expectation I put on myself was how parenting was going to go. You think you can't control a race day? Try to control a toddler. I remember when people used to say to me at work, "Not my circus, not my monkeys." It didn't take long to figure out that being a parent was totally my circus, my monkeys.

It took a couple years, but I finally learned to stop putting expectations on how things would go with the kids. I'm talking vacations, pictures with Santa, birthdays, etc. The things with the kids would go how they would go and I'd best enjoy the ride and not take things so seriously.

When it rains look for rainbows.
When it's dark look for stars.

You know how my first wedding went, my grandmother died. For my second wedding I thought anything would be better than that. I had zero expectations and I am glad, because although we are now divorced, it was a great day. My Dad was just recovering from prostate cancer and my aunt had fallen and broken her hip just two weeks before. For these reasons, we kept the wedding to our immediate family. There were just 9 people.

It was so windy my aunt couldn't stand up. My Dad drove his car across the winery lawn and opened the car door so she could view and listen from the car. That didn't help much because my husband and I were only two feet from the officiator and we couldn't even hear what he was saying due to all the wind. My Dad had an idea to get my aunt's walker out of the trunk. He tossed the large white box that was on top of the walker over to the other side of the trunk. You should have seen his face when I yelled, "Dad! That was the wedding cake!"

We all laughed about the cake and later enjoyed it even though it was all smashed up. The wind made things tricky, but my son loved running in the wind with his jacket flowing behind him like a hero's cape. It wasn't the day we had planned, it was better. A lot of happiness, love, and laughter. The exact right recipe for the perfect day.

I talk about this day because I have had great expectations regarding many of the events I planned for work. That wedding day is a reminder to me that the real success of an event is how the guests feel, not whether the correct plants or flowers are delivered. It is a reminder to go with the universe and not fight it. Our attitudes and reactions can escalate things or diffuse them. Now, my expectations are that we will have a great event, but I don't exactly define what that has to look like.

This brings me to the subject of happiness and how I finally learned it is a choice that we all have.

My 82 year old Dad, my 6 year old daughter, and my 43 year old self were driving in the car one day on the way back from the grocery. It was cloudy and looked like it was going to rain. I looked towards the sky and said, "Shoot! I thought it was going to be a good day." My daughter replied loudly, "It's a great day!"

My Dad looked over at me laughing, "Well that's a lesson for you on perspective." My Dad and his lessons! Who does he think he is with all his now 85 years of wisdom? You would think I would listen to him more.

He has only reminded me about this story like 1,000 times since then. Every time I say something that is not fully positive, he replies, "It's a great day ... if you want it to be."

Well, I have to say I have come around to thinking he is right. My mother has always told me that happiness is a choice. Finally, at age 45 I am ready to believe her. We all have the ability to control the way we react to things and look at things.

Runners learn that some runs will be good and that some runs will not be. People will outwardly judge or criticize our performance. Happiness about our performance and running is up to us, and only us. We control our perspective. Same for life—attitude is a choice.

When I ran that first Olympic Triathlon in August, I felt so elated. I wasn't concerned about any metrics except arriving before the cutoff time. I wanted to see if I could actually do this. When I dropped off the bike and started the run I was thinking, "I am really doing it!" I saw my family on the sidelines, and that gave me so much joy.

I have already said I ran that whole race smiling, except I didn't mention one thing.

When I got off the bike I had numbness in my feet. It was uncomfortable, and really I was just glad that my feet were moving.

The run was a 3.2 mile loop with not much shade that we had to run twice. There was no music allowed. I was just coming in to start the second loop. I had to stay to the left of the finish line where I could see all these other participants completing the race. I wanted to be finishing the race too! I still had over 3 miles to run. I was trying to give myself all the positive self-talk I could muster to do the same exact course again.

I saw my family waving and I had a little burst of energy. I thought, "I'm starting to come back. Dig deep, you can do this." I rounded the corner and took a peep at the mostly now de-serted run course. Then a lady who was near bike maintenance yelled out to me, "Pick up the pace. You're looking slow!" I can only imagine the look I gave her, because she woke up my inner asshole in a major way. In my mind I started thinking, "Oh Bitch, you did not just say that! I ought to leave this course and come clothesline your ass!"

In my head, I kept thinking in some sick way that this person might have been trying to help me, except what she really did is plant a seed of doubt. Now, at this point, I told myself that I can water that seed by being upset or extra critical of myself. Another option was to just not give life to the situation, like it never happened. I was going to, as my friend Lydia likes to say, stay 'unfuckwithable'.

The funny, not-so-funny, thing is that when I was at my next triathlon running up this really gigantic steep hill, I had déjà vu. I had my head down digging deep, thinking that at some point I would get the pleasure of running down this beast of a hill. Right by the top there were two ladies sitting in lawn chairs, and one yelled out, "You are looking slow. Go faster!"

Really? Again? Do I look like I am running in slow motion all the time, or what? In my mind I am running with gazelles. This time my reaction was more like: "Whatever, I am going up a hill." Could someone please explain to this lady that criticizing someone on an otherwise tough mental and physical journey is not helpful? I am just glad that mentally I am in a place to shrug it off. Sometimes people get to me, but that is on me. I can't control them, only my reaction and perspective on the situation. I am trying to focus on making gloomy days great, so I just have to get into my ninja headspace and shrug it off.

"For every minute you are angry, you lose sixty seconds of happiness."—Ralph Waldo Emerson

I was talking to a triathlete about races, life, and attitude. We both have this common goal, which is to be kinder to ourselves. Every day we have the option of focusing on what went wrong, what was just not good enough, OR we have the option to focus on what went right, including things beyond performance (metrics).

WWGS: WHAT WOULD GRANDMA SAY?

She would say, "If you have the choice to see the good or the bad in a situation, why in the world would you ever choose the bad?"

She would say that she was proud of me for challenging myself and wanting more, but she would worry about what that achievement might cost me in terms of stress to myself and others. She would ask me to evaluate if the end justifies the means.

I had a lot of anxiety as a child. I would worry if our house would catch fire, if I would get all my homework done, if I would get made fun of at school the next day. I remember I was lying in bed one night. Grandma was rubbing my back and said, "You are filling your belly full of knots by worrying about so many things. It's not good for you. Everything is going to be fine, so you don't have to worry."

"Worrying means you suffer twice."—Newt Scamander

My grandmother picked me up one day from school in seventh grade. I was crying so hard I could barely speak. I told her I got an F in spelling. I had never had a bad grade before.

She asked to see my report card. She took a pen and made the F into a B. She then said very calmly, "That takes care of that. Don't tell your parents on me." It took me about two seconds to exhale and start laughing with her. "Now we will both be in trouble, Grandma!"

She could always make light of a situation, and let me know that things might be bad now, but they will be good again soon. Do we want to let worry consume us, or do we move on and find a way to choose happiness?

This past week, I read the highlights of a touching conversation someone had with a gentleman in a wheelchair that illustrated great perspective. A person once asked the gentleman if it was difficult to be confined to a wheelchair. He responded, "I'm not confined to my wheelchair—I am liberated by it. If it wasn't for my wheelchair, I would be bed-bound and never able to leave my room or house."

Some people look at a field of dandelions and see 100 weeds. Some see 1,000 wishes.

"Happiness lies in perspective."

"When I was 5 years old, my mother told me that happiness was the key to life. When I went to school, they asked me what I wanted to be when I grew up. I wrote down 'happy'. They told me I didn't understand the assignment, and I told them that they didn't understand life."
—John Lennon

PLAN to CHANGE

A friend recently woke up ready to do a half-Ironman distance race, but once he got there things didn't go as planned. The water was very choppy and somehow he missed buoys. He knew that his times would be disqualified. He could have continued with the rest of the race for the heck of it, but instead he decided to pull out of the race and switch to the sprint distance race they had that day.

In the end, it wasn't the day he trained for, but he was 8th overall in the sprint and won his age group.

A couple hours after this happened, he messaged me:

Him: "It was a tough call, I hope it was the right one!"

Me: "It was! Don't second guess yourself. I do that too, and it's a waste of good head space. You did the best you could in the moment. And now you go on to the next!"

Him: "Exactly. My coach said he is proud of me."

Me: "Of course! You did awesome! What would you say to me if I did exactly what you did?"

Him: "You made the right the call."

Me: "Yep!"

There is a saying:

You can't control the wind, but you can adjust the sails.

My type A personality needs to really embrace this saying. I become locked in, I'm talking laser-focused, on a goal. Everything wrong could be going on, and the best thing to do is to change course. But no, there I go running straight into the wind making things more difficult on myself and sometimes others. Some would call this 'being stubborn'.

It has taken me a lot of years to get to the point of self-awareness, to realize that there are bigger goals in life that supersede my sports goals. In the end, I have to ask myself, "Why am I doing this?" Getting too caught up in goals sometimes blinds me to the best decisions, which might be to get off the course and go on a new route.

All of this talk about, "Don't be a quitter" and "Stay determined," is good to a point unless things get totally unreasonable. It's at that point where I have to totally un-brainwash myself from the coaching that was given to me as a kid in the 80s.

Running has taught me that I will be in constant frustration if I don't learn to quickly change expectations as circumstances change. This is totally necessary for me to guarantee that I both have a successful run and finish with good feelings … we are supposed to be having fun right?!

There is a distinction between quitting and changing plans. The majority of runners I know have been faced with each of these decisions at some point, in some way, because as much as we plan and try, we can't control the race. Mistakes or accidents happen, they WILL happen. I have learned that these issues make for the best stories later, so at least there is that.

While writing this book, I had the pleasure to interview Jack Taunton. This is a man who has done everything it seems, and as a runner he has logged over 120,000 miles.

He told me about a memorable run he had in preparation for the New York City Marathon with a gentleman he was pacing. Their practice run was one of the ones he said you wish you could capture, because it felt effortless.

On the day of the NYC Marathon he was well prepared, and had a solid plan. Jack was running with his friend Jack Foster, whose goal was to break the world record for a male over 50 (2:17).

During the race, they were on pace until mile 20. Coming off the Queensboro Bridge another runner fell into a pothole. Jack fell over him. His friend ran on, and so did Jack, except now he had a broken pelvis. Jack did not make the time he wanted, but he somehow miraculously finished the race despite this huge setback. He also had amazing stories about people he talked to while running those last 6 miles!

In so many races, I have had this idealistic thought of what the race would look like, and then ... life. Cue Mother Nature to show up with unexpected humidity, wind, or rain. Cue the brain fart that left some of my gear at home. Cue the unpredictability of animals, people, and hardware. Cue my stomach to fight back against my body.

There is this saying: "We plan, and God laughs." I am learning to laugh at these moments, too. As I mature, I spend less time dwelling in disappointment and more time focusing on what is next. *Sometimes it takes coaching from others to get me there.*

I read a story yesterday about a woman who was doing her first IronMan event. There is a lot of training, nerves, and anticipation that revolves around this event. After all her training, planning, and expenses to get to the race, during her race, she stopped to administer CPR to someone along the course. Being a RN, she said she never hesitated to do what needed to be done.

She saved someone's life. She didn't finish the race. I'm certain that in all her planning she didn't think once about that scenario. What a blessing it was for that person, that she was in the very place where they needed help. I would call this good luck, not bad luck.

Later, I heard that the famous Mike Riley, who calls people's names out at the finish line as they cross and announces they are an IronMan, called her directly and told her that she was an IronMan. Talk about a moving story!

So many times I look back on my life and think, "Thank goodness things didn't go according to my plan."

I am sure that when you hear Jack's story about running on a broken pelvis you might think he needs to learn "to adjust the sails." The thing is, Jack's story is all about adjusting, and in his words "reinventing himself."

When life shuts a door ... open it again. It's a door.
That's how they work.

He never planned to be a runner. He had polio as a child, and just as he was recovering he was hit by a car. He wasn't even able to play sports until age 16. He was told at that time he would never be able to run.

His focus was on soccer and football. He did some short distance track running, but it wasn't until his dreams of playing professional football fell through in college that he started to focus on running.

While some of us were thinking about what we want to eat for dinner during our run, Jack was chasing a 2:20 marathon time. His dream was to run a marathon in the Olympics.

During the Olympic trials he was in third place with only a mile to go when he collapsed from heat stroke. He said he finally fulfilled his dreams of going to the Olympics years later, through the back door as their Chief Medical Officer. "This gave me the opportunity to be part of 8 Olympics. I made it in a different sort of a way."

I would say the one thing you can't say to Jack Taunton is, "You can't do this." Despite stories of heat strokes, genetic spine issues, dyslexia, broken pelvises, and heart problems, he has continually found ways to re-engineer his goals and persevere, and many times in an even better way!

Jack's life passion has revolved around running. "Running has given me everything." Had he gone on with football or just given up entirely instead of changing course, he may never had done some of the incredible things he has done, including co-founding the Vancouver Marathon and the Sun Run. Those races get 23,000 and 60,000 people running each race, respectively.

"Sometimes good things fall apart, so better things can fall together."—Marilyn Monroe

I follow @runningquotes and loved this: "My running journey is a path of courage, defeat, dreams, grit, success, setback, forward leaps, and love." I think I could describe my life in the very same way.

The setbacks and defeats are how we grow. Someone once said, "Failure is good. It's fertilizer. Everything I've learned, I've learned from making mistakes."

This chapter isn't so much about failure or mistakes, but how runners and athletes in general learn to quickly adapt to new plans. In the moment, you have no choice but to embrace the will to change and move on.

There is an understanding that those runs and races where everything is perfect do not happen all the time. When they do, it's super special. When they don't, you look for ways to recover and make them special—even if this new special looks entirely different than what we had anticipated.

Working with people in office settings who say they can't change, but desire change, makes me often think of this: "For something to change, something has to change."

Having been through this sudden 'change of plans' so many times in running has given me new flexibility in my personal life.

Change has always been hard for me, but the older I get the more fortunate I feel to have the option to change. This quote has been so powerful for me:

"If you ever find yourself in the wrong story … leave."

I have thought about not being happy in marriage at the age of 42, and thought, "If I have twice my life to live, *let's be hopeful*, then is this how I want it to be? Do I want my kids to see me living in tension and turmoil?" What really resonated with me is when I asked myself, "Do my kids deserve to have happy parents and a happy home life?"

Every day, we have the opportunity to write our own story. So … if I am not happy, then that is on me. "Happiness is always a change away."

My son was in a school he loved. However, he started to struggle with reading and spelling in first grade. That year, he was diagnosed with dyslexia. The school made a lot of accommodations to work with him into second grade.

I will never forget driving to the school because they needed to speak with me about my son. They brought me into a room full of teachers and explained to me that they could no longer meet the needs of my son, and that he would be best off at another school.

There are two things that got me through that moment. One, only moments before the meeting I had lunch with my son and his friends in the school cafeteria. His sweet friend Brian looked at me and out of the blue said, "I think Jack Hall has the best mom he could have for him." To this day, that may be the sweetest and most sincere compliment I have ever been given!

Two, I chose that school because I knew they would never let my kid slip through the cracks of the system. They knew they couldn't meet his needs and they were upfront about that. It was hard to hear, but in the end I had to praise them for serving my child in the best way possible, although it would be tough on him.

My son's heart was broken. He told me he hated himself and that he was stupid. We went through a tremendous struggle trying to find a school. He had a lot of tears, and behind closed doors I had a lot of tears too. His self-esteem got so low during that time.

All I could do was to have faith in him and get him to a place that would understand him, nurture him, and teach him in a way that he could learn. A place that would allow him to be and feel successful. This search was not easy, but we finally found a place at The dePaul School in Louisville, KY. Within months, my son was so much better.

"All great changes are preceded by chaos."
—Deepak Chopra

Never regret a day in your life. Good days give happiness. Bad days give experience. Worst days give lessons, and best days give memories.

A full year later, my son told me that he was so glad he changed schools. We talked about how proud I was of his perseverance. I told him I hoped he gained strength in what happened and confidence to know that he can endure through tough times in life. Things get better and change is not our enemy.

As Warren Buffet said, "In a chronically leaking boat, energy devoted to changing vessels is more productive than energy devoted to patching leaks."

WWGS: WHAT WOULD GRANDMA SAY?
She would probably say, "Isn't it nice to even be able to have the choice to change? Go where the wind (heart) takes you, and have fun with that."

KEEP *learning*

About 10 years ago I was at a meeting for work. They had this exercise involving photo cards. There were maybe around 200 of these photo cards spread out over a table. The task was for us to pick 2 to 4 cards and tell a story.

Some people randomly selected cards and then created their own story. Others spent a great deal of time pouring over the photos looking for just the right photos. Honestly, I don't remember what I did. What I do remember very clearly is my colleague from another country. It was her turn to share. She placed down a picture of the sun, then one of rain, and then one of plants. She said simply, "Sun plus rain equals growth."

I was so touched. I thought it was simply beautiful. Afterwards, I told her I thought that her statement was a great metaphor for life and that I loved it. She replied, "What?" Oh, I thought she was going deep with life, but apparently she meant all of it in a very literal sense. I decided I didn't care. I wrote "Sun + Rain = Growth" down on a napkin and hung it at my workstation.

This simple edict reminds me that when things get tough, there is always a chance for growth. I want to remember that each season I should grow as a person. I need to appreciate the times of light and the times of rain as part of this process. This is how true growth is achieved.

I have heard there is no age limit to learning and growing as a person. In contrast to, "You can't teach an old dog new tricks," I have found that the older my friends and I get the more we realize that maybe we don't know that much after all.

I read an article that asked readers the question, "What is something someone said that forever changed your way of thinking?" A gentleman named Henry said that when he was in his late thirties, he was contemplating going to school for a two-year degree. He had almost talked himself out of doing it thinking he was too old. He told his friend, "I'll be 40 when I get my degree." His friend said "If you don't do it, you'll still be 40, but without the degree." He is nearly 60 now, and that degree has been the difference between making a decent living, and struggling to get by.

I have a friend who is now in his 40s. He is an elite cyclist for a local team. One day we were talking about running and cycling and he mentioned I should get a running coach.

My gut reaction was, "Why do I need a running coach? I'm not planning on winning any races."

He was telling me about all the things that the coaches do for them: how to schedule training, when to rest, when to push yourself, nutrition, avoiding injury, and being more efficient in your sport. It's not simply about going faster. My friend Andy echoed his points in another conversation, and felt that if I was going to just jump into triathlons so quickly, coaching would be the best way possible for me to avoid injury.

I spent a lot of time thinking about this. Elite athletes, even in their 40s, use coaches. They are still willing to learn from an expert and other teammates, and this learning extends beyond the sport and into their lifestyle. This also tells me that the learning process never truly ends for an athlete.

I do love learning things from running boards, groups, and just general conversations. There is always an opportunity to have that a-ha moment or evolve.

I finally decided to take my friends up on their advice. I started with a swimming coach, Mike Jotautas. I learned so much from the first session. Apparently, people are supposed to exhale under water and inhale when they turn their head. I was holding my breath. A simple adjustment in my breathing while swimming immediately increased my comfort and endurance.

I was able to speed up the learning curve by leaps and bounds. Which is good, since I only had about a third of the typical time people spend to train for a triathalon.

Next, I decided to enlist the help of a cycle coach, Curtis Tolson, for road bike training. I had long been scared of cycling, so working with Curtis helped to reduce a lot of my anxiety.

It was through this process of working with coaches and really actively seeking out help that I realized how little I actually knew about training AND running. I wondered where I would be now in running if I had sought help years ago. Ironically, the most dramatic improvements I have ever made in running came after I started following training plans given to me by Curtis—at age 45!

"Never stop learning because life never stops teaching."
—Unknown

This is what I now know. I have enough material to write a set of books on what I have done wrong in running and life. More than half of this book is based on my evolution to where I am now, brought on by a series of stupid mistakes and turning a blind eye to the obvious.

In the future, I will work to learn more from others and not by being the one who gets to announce to the group: "If you don't unclip both bike pedals, you might fall over." "If you don't get the chlorine out of your hair, it might turn green." Or, "If you give kids cans of silly string, you might want to google how to remove it from your hair and flesh."

At various points in my life I have taken the perspective that it is too late for me to make changes, learn, improve, or even win. But this is simply a perspective thing, and what would happen if I asked for help more?

There are two things my Dad taught me in business. First, no one ever went broke making a profit. Second, and most importantly, listen to experts and get their help when possible.

Have I made mistakes by not following these two things? Yes. Did that lesson help me learn how valuable the advice really was? Absolutely!

When I wanted to write a book I started out alone. I didn't know what I was doing besides just writing. I thought that I would eventually figure it out. However, when the opportunity to have expert guidance presented itself, I went with my gut and my Dad's advice.

I am not ever going to proclaim to have the best book. I will never be that confident in myself. I am still (somewhat) embarrassed that I actually wrote a book! I am not sure why this is how I feel, except that maybe it won't be good enough to meet the expectations of others and that I don't want to disappoint anyone.

What I will proclaim though, is that I have had the best and most supportive mentors. It takes special people to handle a person like myself who is one day super driven and the next crawling under the covers saying they can't face the world. When I surround myself with positive people who know what they are doing AND I listen to them, things always go better for me.

WWGS: WHAT WOULD GRANDMA SAY?

She would say, "Ann Wilson! I already told you all you needed to know, but you weren't listening!" She would say talk less, and listen more. Actually, my Dad has often said that if I could manage to keep my mouth shut and my ears open, half my problems would disappear!

"God gave us mouths that close and ears that don't, that must tell us something."—Eugene O'Neill

PIT STOP

WHAT IS THE BEST RUNNING ADVICE YOU HAVE EVER RECEIVED? WHAT HAS BEEN A KEY LEARNING MOMENT IN RUNNING? CAN YOU APPLY ANY LESSONS LEARNED IN RUNNING TO LIFE?

When I first started running, I naively thought that the person who will win the race will be the fittest. I took the mental out of the equation, and I also neglected the role of the heart.

My favorite cartoon is *Heart and Brain* by the Awkward Yeti. The drawings illustrate the ongoing battle between the carefree heart and the logical brain. This battle continually plays out in all areas of my life. The heart wants what it wants, reasonable or not.

What I have learned is that heart will always win. It determines the amount of passion we put into what we do. That passion is the ultimate rocket fuel, right? It is the difference between giving just enough, and giving more than we ever thought possible.

The best running advice I have ever received I saw on a poster board during a 13.1 mile race. It said, "When your legs give out, run with your heart."

I can truly say my best races are indeed the ones where my heart took over. They were the most fulfilling, good metrics or not. When you let your heart lead, you never lose.

Now, when people ask me, "What pace do you run?" I simply respond, "Whatever my heart will allow."

Another favorite saying of mine is, "Try to be a faster you."

Here is some of the game-changing advice my friends have received along the way:

Jaclyn, 35; Salem, MA

Trust your training and breathe. All of those miles put in the past few months are going to help guide you to the finish line. Take it one step at a time, one breath at a time.

Relax. Running isn't supposed to be stressful. There will always be another chance, another race, another training session. Stressing isn't going to make you feel better. Focus on what you are doing, then worry about tomorrow, next week, next month. If something was so important that needed to be done, you wouldn't be running right now!

Krishna, 33; Holland, MI

Push through the first 20 minutes no matter how much you don't want to, the end result is amazing. In life don't give up on your goals just because of the initial challenges.

Mike, 36; Dayton, OH

Some of the best advice I have been given in running is that you don't have to run every run at race pace. Focus on running consistent.

You have to run certain runs at certain higher thresholds, while others are slower. Not all of your runs have to be at X min miles. This taught me a lot. For the first time, in March 2018, I ran a marathon PR of 3:20 and all of my miles were practically even. That said a lot, considering I never ran like this before.

I have also learned through training with my friend Doug to not go out too hard during a race. It's one of the ways you can ruin a race—giving too much, too soon.

Lucy, 54; Louisville, KY

A key moment in running for me was when I learned, "Do NOT let anyone put limits on YOU … it's YOUR life!

I jumped in and started running cross-country for Eastern High School as a sophomore in Kentucky. I loved it. However at that time women were only 'allowed' to run a 3K in high school cross-country competitions. I was so frustrated. It felt to me, that just as I was getting warmed up, I reached the finish line and had to stop. I asked the coach why I couldn't run longer races and was told that women are 'too fragile'. This seemed strange, as I had gone for a 10 mile run just the day before.

In the early 90's, a potential surgeon told me, when I had tarsel tunnel in both feet, that I most likely would never run again, much less fulfill my dream of completing a marathon. I used a different surgeon, and put both these myths to rest.

I have since completed over 12,000 running miles and 12 marathons, of which the last two were at the end of full 140.6 mile Ironman races. I completed the Boston Marathon, by the grace of God, in 1996 when my youngest was 2.

So … listen to others negative opinions with a grain of salt. We make our own positive choices about what we can do.

I feel that this choice, this applies to our lives, as well. We are all given talents and gifts to use, that light us up inside. We should strive to seek and have jobs and hobbies that light us up while also challenging us.

Others may give advice from their life perspective, and it is important to listen to others, however, it is YOUR life and YOU need to sort through and make your own choices about what you want to do, and how you are going to live.

Are you going to let someone say something that stops you from reaching for your dreams, or let negative mindsets creep in? You can say, "What IF?" But, "What IF YOU CAN?????"

In my story: "The only failing is not trying." —Lucy Monin

Thomas, 48; Lexington, KY

I think the key to enjoying running is to figure out what you want to do and then make it work for you. There are some people that love to stick with the quicker 5K distances, and that is fine. Once you find what brings you joy, then surround yourself with like-minded people.

There are people out there that never want to get off the couch. They can bring you down. They can try to convince you to eat unhealthily, stay up late, cut your workouts short, and really anything else that can derail you. You need to counter those influences with supportive people who understand what you are working to do.

You will learn from like-minded people. You may be sitting around drinking a beer, and they may say one little tidbit that can push you to the next level in your journey. You might help them, too.

In regards to running and life, we all have a purpose in life. We all have a calling in life, no matter what it is. I get a lot of people who tell me that I inspire them. I just turned 48 years old and people will say, "It amazes me that you are still out there running, and running the way that you do." I think running makes me a better person. It makes me want to do better. In life, I always want to be positive. I don't want people to look at me and think I am up to no good. I want them to look at me and think, "Look at Thomas, he is setting a good example."

I don't know how long I will be able to do this. I am going to do this until my body says I can't do it anymore. If I can continue to inspire this way, then that is what I am going to do.

finish STRONG

13

Both my sisters ran cross country for a couple of years in elementary and middle school. Alice had really long legs and the coach said she was a natural. Mary, on the opposite end of the spectrum, had short legs and seemed to have to fight for every mile.

I can very vividly remember watching Mary run. We were always somewhere waiting for her to appear amongst the last of the runners.

The best memory I have is standing with my mom and another mother watching kids run in to the finish line. The other mom said, "I see Nate and Mary!" I couldn't spot them. She pointed to a giant bush about a quarter of a mile from the finish. Through the thin branches of the bush you could see them hunched down with their hands on their knees.

Nate's mom said, "Looks like they're taking a break." Of course, the two of them had no idea that any of the spectators could see them. After about two minutes or so they stood up and positioned themselves in a running stance. Two seconds later they both took off running as fast as they could towards the finish line.

They looked strong and fast, and if you hadn't seen their rest break you might have been under the illusion that this is how they looked the whole race.

I wasn't a runner then and didn't give much thought to it, except for the fact that I found it really funny. I had no idea at the time the difficulty of that course and what it took for them just to make it to that very spot.

Today, I love to stand at the finish line, cheer, and people watch. It is such a great feeling to know you are almost done and that you've made it.

If you stand farther back along the course, you can see people going along. Once they eye that finish line and all the spectators, their whole demeanor changes! Their pace quickens, and they get this look of determination. So many will start a sprint right as they are coming up to the line of spectators cheering. It's like there is a fire underneath them. I'm the same!

My last race I was running so hard at the finish line I actually peed myself—darn mom bladder! Guess what? I continued smiling because I had made it!

No matter how much pain or how tired people are, even if they have walked the majority of the race, runners tend to pull out their very best at the end to finish strong.

One of the ultimate skills to have is to be able to pace yourself, where your last half of the race can be your fastest and strongest. You specifically want enough gas left in the tank to run to the finish line strong.

This concept seems easy enough, but in my experience it is super tough. Hold back too much and have too much left in the tank in the end, and you feel like you could have done more and that you didn't give your best. Run too hard, too fast, and you will be fighting for every step in the end.

Those races when you get it exactly right are pure magic! I now try to approach life with the goal to finish strong. The perfect amount of effort at the right time, to present your best. It all circles back to pace. How great it feels at the end of the day knowing you accomplished all the things you needed to do, and are not totally spent.

I have started a few too many things in my life with much gusto, but then start to fade when the going gets tough or monotonous. Somewhere along the line, the project loses its new fun and challenging appeal, and I look for excuses to move on to something else. Sounds almost like a running race: the last half of a long race is where things get uncomfortable. It's where I might contemplate walking or giving up all together.

What keeps me running in a race? I have made a commitment to complete the race, and quite frankly how else am I going to get home? Once you are out on the course you are pretty much locked into doing the race. Also, who wants to tell their friends, "I quit the race because it got tough."

This book has been one of these projects where I have doubted my ability to move forward and finish. I have questioned if I was good enough or worthy of telling a story. It got uncomfortable and difficult.

Without even knowing it, I created my own race scenario. I brought in coaches for accountability and guidance. I told co-workers, friends, and family I was writing a book. I locked myself in because the only way out would be telling everyone that I gave up because it got too hard.

If running has taught me anything, it is that this is the time to dig deep. These are the hours to put in the real work. These are the times my mind is going to scramble for a way out, and that I have to let heart take over. Heart, for me in running and in life, is the one thing that will propel me forward. Find the passion and the reason I am doing these things in the first place and I will emerge from those bushes just shy of the finish line like I am running an Olympic pace time.

I am not going to dwell on how much time I spent in those bushes just outside of the finish line trying to gather the mental strength to power through with this book. At this point, that was simply part of the process. I needed a pit stop and a few others to get me to this place. This place I am at now is where I can visualize that finish line. I am sprinting with gusto!

I might tear up here, because when the journey became uncomfortable I can think about what helped drive me to get to this very spot:

The fear of not finishing was far worse than continuing on. I promised my grandmother I would write this story. She was not alive to hear that promise, but I made it—to her.

"Starting strong is good. Finishing stong is epic."
—Robin Sharma

WWGS: WHAT WOULD GRANDMA SAY?
"I knew that you could do it Ann Wilson! You are almost there! Keep going!"

BREATHE

I don't care if it is a 5K or a full marathon, there is nothing like that feeling of finally crossing the finish line. That moment you can finally catch a breath. It's like almost immediately you turn off fighting the challenge of the race.

If you have run a race, you know it. The deep exhale as you slow your pace down to a walk. All the torment of the run is so distant, yet it just happened. As you crossed that line the torment was instantly replaced with a great sense of accomplishment, confirming that you indeed weathered the storm.

Your new focus is just to breathe. It is the time to trade the stress and impact of running for the relief of recovery. It is a very defined and purposeful time to stop the race, rest, refuel … take a moment. The perfect time for reflection, to appreciate all you have just done.

It's too bad we don't have these clearly defined finish lines in real life. I guess sometimes we do, I can think of graduation as one example. That milestone has been done and celebrated.

What I am talking about though is everyday life. Last week, you had parent teacher conferences, unexpected house guests, a big project for work, and a tree limb down in the yard. As you were racing through that week, you went straight into the next week. There might have been a finish line in sight, so to speak, but you just buzzed right through it to start the next race. There was no purposeful time to slow down, breathe, and just simply take a moment to recover.

When I say you, I guess what I really mean is me. This is how I am, a lot. For too long, I have been working on changing. Even after months of gaining this new awareness that I need to slow my pace and apply basic running principles to my life, I still struggle to pull it all together.

It's okay though. It took me a while in running to figure out pace. Remember when I was trying to chaotically sprint the long races? There is nothing as humbling as having someone about 30 years older than you and 30 pounds heavier than you pass you as if they are gliding on air. Meanwhile, I was struggling just to breathe and walk at the same time.

Guess what? They know. Experience has taught them the important of pace. They know when to go full force, and when to pull back. They probably also know that it's a race and so it's not to be taken so fucking seriously.

Hmmm ... is this the same in life? Perhaps I just shouldn't take it so seriously, *still deep appreciation for life or maybe even deeper appreciation for life, actually.* I know how to win at running. I mean technically I'm not winning, but I can clearly see the defined rules on how to win a race.

But how do I win in life? Certainly it is not determined by the speed that I zip through it. Doesn't that oftentimes lead to a shorter race? This is just some last 'food for thought'.

Where can I carve out these finish lines in life so I can have a moment to breathe, look back at my journey, and see how far I have come, what I have endured?

Taking it down to the most basic level, "How can I carve some defined finish lines into my week?" *Please do not say "yoga!" Dammit! I knew you were going to say that. Hahaha, I will consider it.*

For now, I am going to go back in time about 50 years and start having a rest day on Sunday. I don't know how 'stuff' is going to get done, but I think it will. Yep, Sunday is my now finish line day, dedicated to doing fun stuff and recovery. Let's consider it my weekly post-race bash.

Since I am a working single mom of two kids, clearly this can't happen every Sunday, but I'm going to try for most. Perhaps my situation actually dictates that I need the rest day more than ever. If I don't rest that day, then when? Please don't say when I am dead. I would like to think that I might have the possibility to exhale before then.

There is this saying:

"If you want to change your body, run. If you want to change your life, run a marathon."

Please allow me to change this saying a bit.

If you want to change your body, run. If you want to change your life, apply basic running principles to your life: Find motivation, Show up, Enjoy the Moment, Pace Yourself, Take Rest, Quiet the Mind, Put People First, Imagine Success, Plan to Change, Choose Happiness, Value Fit, Form and Nutrition, Watch Expectations, Keep Learning, Challenge Yourself, Finish Strong—AND DON'T FORGET TO BREATHE!

This has been my take on running and life. Of course I would love to hear yours. *Am I going to regret saying that?!* Find me in your favorite social media platform at ErgoRunner.

GROUP MEET-UP: WHAT IS THE BEST THING THAT RUNNING HAS TAUGHT YOU? WHAT HAS IT GIVEN YOU?

Well, I think I just about covered my perspectives in the previous chapters. It only took me 2 years and over 50,000 words! In all seriousness, it has been a journey of love even when I was fighting against the process of running *and writing!*

It has been one of my great pleasures to write this book and share it with you. In this last pit stop, I would like to leave you with some key insights from other runners, mentors, and friends.

As they say in my favorite movie: "So long, farewell, auf wiedersehen, goodbye!"

Jaclyn, 35; Salem, MA

Mind over matter. You know when your body is failing you. Most of the time you make up excuses that you 'can't', when really you just aren't being mentally tough. I've definitely become more mentally tough over the past year while training for my marathon. Ten miles seemed like a distance I would never be able to run without some kind of support, whether it be a group run or a race. The first time I ran that far by myself, I knew I could conquer any distance. I knew I could physically do it, since I had done it many times before, but never alone. Running long distances alone had been the biggest mental challenge for me, but now I know I can do it and the distance doesn't intimidate me anymore.

Running has given me a better purpose and allowed me to become part of an amazing community. Once I started running, I realized I was actually good at it. I'm a pretty competitive person, mostly with myself, and I like to challenge myself to be better, to be faster, but to also enjoy myself. There have been many people who have helped me enjoy running more, and I've also developed life-long friendships in the process.

I was in a very bad place when I started running, and if had never met my friend Tammy and my coach Martin at my first Team In Training group run I probably would have never gone back. They were so welcoming and supportive that I looked forward to every bi-weekly group meeting. Each week, I would meet new people and I eventually became part of the community of runners in the area. Even though I moved out of the area a few years ago, I still keep in touch with many of them and continue to run races with them. Since moving, I have now found a group of runners that have brought me into their running community, which made the transition much easier. Without either of these amazing running communities, I would not have met some of my closest friends and made amazing memories that I will never forget.

Mike, 36; Dayton, OH

What I have learned through running is to not give up. It's possible to inspire many people and live how you are supposed to, or want to, live. You never know who is watching, and trust me, people see what you do even if you don't know it. It's an amazing feeling to hear a random person tell you how much you have inspired them.

Running has given me confidence in myself and provided me with a purpose. It gave me a reason to keep moving forward, and I always look at it as it putting more distance between how I used to be and who I am now.

Krishna, 33; Holland, MI

Pacing myself to my own ability. It's my gateway to independence and also my gateway to making my personal relationships deeper.

Lucy, 54: Louisville, KY

Don't give up when it gets hard, keep moving forward because as you put in the training your body will adapt and it will get easier.

This concept applies to life as well. Sometimes when it gets tough, you have to decide how bad you want it.

Running brought me confidence when I was in those awkward teen years. It helped me channel my energy and feel like there was something I was good at. It made me 'unique' and different in a great way!

Running has given me courage and confidence to go after my dreams. It has brought amazing people into my life. It has brought wonderful stories of other's journeys as we run together sharing time and the gift of running. It has brought me so much happiness. Running also teaches me to challenge myself, which gave me the courage to go after another dream—to become an Ironman!

Sarah, 45; Portland, OR

For me, running has taught me that I'm stronger than I think. That I can do more than I realize, if I put my mind to it. I often go out now with a distance in mind. I push myself to go farther when I'm feeling good. I've learned that you should keep going because sometimes it takes a while to hit that comfort zone, the one where you feel like you can go forever.

Running has given me back the playfulness of being a kid again, especially when I can run in the rain and splash through the puddles, or do fartleks with my friends. Running in the rain is so cathartic. It seems to wash away my troubles. It's very rare for me to finish a run where I don't feel good mentally.

Thomas, 48; Lexington, KY

Running has taught me to be more disciplined. If you want to be a successful runner you have to put in the work, and that takes discipline. When you have a long day or you don't feel like doing the running, you have to get through that and do what needs to be done. You also have to have discipline with your nutrition. You have to give your body the right fuel that it needs to perform. Today at work they had donuts. I wanted one, but I knew that it would affect my 8 mile run later. When you are training, it teaches you to listen to your body and make choices that will benefit your body.

RESOURCES

1. "The Power of Writing Down Your Hopes and Dreams" (2016). Mary Morrissey. Huffpost

2. Rath, Tom (2013). *Eat, Move, Sleep*. MissionDay

3. Presentation: "Keeping Employees Energised and Increasing their Efficiency" (2014). Stefan IJmker PhD

4. "The American State of Vacation" (2017). Project Time Off

5. "Americans not taking vacation, and it hurts" (2012), David Weinberg. Marketplace.

6. "Daydream your way to Success." Really (2012). Monica Mehta. Inc.

7. Doidge, Norman (2007). *The Brain that Changes Itself*. Penguin Books

8. "Seeing is Believing: The Power of Visualization" (2009). AJ Adams. Psychology Today

9. Neuropsychologia. 2004;42(7):944-56. "From mental power to muscle power—gaining strength by using the mind." Ranganathan VK1, Siemionow V, Liu JZ, Sahgal V, Yue GH.

10. "Seven Ways Meditation Can Actually Change the Brain" (2015). Alice Walton. Forbes

Made in the USA
Columbia, SC
20 January 2020